Cambridge Elements

Elements in the Problems of God
edited by
Michael L. Peterson
Asbury Theological Seminary

EMBODIMENT, DEPENDENCE, AND GOD

Kevin Timpe
Calvin University

Shaftesbury Road, Cambridge CB2 8EA, United Kingdom

One Liberty Plaza, 20th Floor, New York, NY 10006, USA

477 Williamstown Road, Port Melbourne, VIC 3207, Australia

314–321, 3rd Floor, Plot 3, Splendor Forum, Jasola District Centre,
New Delhi – 110025, India

103 Penang Road, #05–06/07, Visioncrest Commercial, Singapore 238467

Cambridge University Press is part of Cambridge University Press & Assessment,
a department of the University of Cambridge.

We share the University's mission to contribute to society through the pursuit of education, learning and research at the highest international levels of excellence.

www.cambridge.org
Information on this title: www.cambridge.org/9781009500401

DOI: 10.1017/9781009270052

When citing this work, please include a reference to the DOI 10.1017/9781009270052

First published 2024

A catalogue record for this publication is available from the British Library.

ISBN 978-1-009-50040-1 Hardback
ISBN 978-1-009-27007-6 Paperback
ISSN 2754-8724 (online)
ISSN 2754-8716 (print)

Embodiment, Dependence, and God

Elements in the Problems of God

DOI: 10.1017/9781009270052
First published online: November 2024

Kevin Timpe
Calvin University

Author for correspondence: Kevin Timpe, kevin.timpe@calvin.edu

Abstract: The significance of our physical bodies is an important topic in contemporary philosophy and theology. Reflection on the body often assumes, even if only implicitly, idealizations that obscure important facts about what it means for humans to be "enfleshed." This Element explores a number of ways that reflection on bodies in their concrete particularities is important. It begins with a consideration of why certain forms of idealization are philosophically problematic. It then explores how a number of features of bodies can reveal important truths about human nature, embodiment, and dependence. Careful reflection on the body raises important questions related to community and interdependence. The Element concludes by exploring the ethical demands we face given human embodiment. Among other results, this Element exposes the reader to a wide diversity of human embodiment and the nature of human dependence, encouraging meaningful theological reflection on aspects of the human condition.

Keywords: embodiment, dependence, disability, bodies, vulnerability

JEL classifications: A12, B34, C56, D78, E90

ISBNs: 9781009500401 (HB), 9781009270076 (PB), 9781009270052 (OC)
ISSNs: 2754-8724 (online), 2754-8716 (print)

Contents

1 The Importance of Embodiment

1.1 Overview

Part of what it means to be human is to have a body, to *be* embodied. We live as embodied beings. As theologian Marjorie Suchocki writes, we humans "are *we*: social beings, living in interaction with others like us. We are embodied creatures, with a distinctive human anatomy that endows us with certain restraints. We require food, air, water, and a certain degree of temperature in order to live. We are mortal in that we die" (Suchocki 1994, 49). Our lives are complex webs of embodied experiences, actions, and habits. As we'll see in the coming pages, our relationship with our embodiment is complicated. While our bodies are always present, they sometimes drop out of our active consideration and recede into the background. At other times, we take them seriously, but tend to do so under various kinds of idealization. Both of these tendencies are understandable. Yet these tendencies can both be problematic, especially if we are not aware of exactly what we're doing when we engage in them. Furthermore, humans are social creatures and members of moral communities. The fact that humans are embodied in the ways we are places certain normative demands on us that we'll explore later. But let's begin with the fact that we often take facets of our embodiment for granted.

Consider the fact that often that our embodiment recedes into the background. We know that we need to eat, sleep, and bathe. But it's easy for us to live our lives without thinking explicitly about our bodies, even though much of what we experience, think about, and know comes through our bodies. For instance, we experience and know about our environment through our senses. I can hear the ascending and descending scale of the violin in Arvo Pärt's *Spiegal im Spiegal* as I type in my office. We know about our bodies through interoception and proprioception. I know that my left foot is asleep, having sat at my desk typing with my legs crossed too long. Even when we notice our bodies, our knowledge of them is limited. Our hip flexor might scream for our attention upon leaving the gym, even though we didn't notice whatever we did that caused it to hurt. We might not know that our tibia is developing osteomyelitis until we finally experience extreme bone pain. Much of our body is hidden from our own experience without the aid of medical testing. Are you aware of the internal positioning or health of your gall bladder at present?

Much of our life is lived in what philosopher Drew Leder calls "the corporeal absence" (Leder 1990, 1). We often don't notice our bodies, even while we use them. We don't notice the feel of socks on our feet until something draws it to our conscious attention (Ratliffe 2008). Until this sentence, you might not have been aware of the pressure on your fingers from holding this Element or your Kindle. You likely weren't thinking about the rhythm of your breathing, the rise and fall of your chest. Our bodies fall away from our conscious experience, much as we don't pay explicit attention to the shape of the individual letters in the words on the page when reading. There are some tasks that we can only do, or do best, when our bodies recede from our conscious awareness in this way. Thinking about the contraction of individual muscles, such as exactly how high we need to raise our leg by flexing the iliopsoas muscle, gets in the way of walking up the stairs rather than facilitates the process. We play the violin best when the need to pay attention to exact finger positioning on the fingerboard, as when we first learned, and the flexing of our wrist and arm moving the bow fades from our focus. We can lose ourselves in the music rather than specifics of our bodies.

Approaching the lack of explicit attention to the body from another direction, philosopher Alasdair MacIntyre writes that much philosophical reflection is "forgetful of the body" precisely by being overly focused on rationality, as if that is "somehow independent of our animality" (MacIntyre 1999, 5). This hyper-rationalistic focus is not only true of much philosophy but also within religion. Sometimes this is expressed in the tendency, found especially among some contemporary philosophers of religion, to have an overly cognitive approach that focuses on beliefs about religious doctrines rather than embodied religious practices. James K. A. Smith, for instance, thinks that much contemporary philosophy of religion is characterized by "a lingering rationalism which remains at least haunted (if not perhaps *governed*) by a Cartesian anthropology that tends to construe the human person as, in essence, a 'thinking thing'" (Smith 2021, 15). This tendency can encourage us to "leave the body behind," for instance, when thinking about the afterlife as if we became disembodied angels rather than continue to be the embodied humans that we are, albeit redeemed.

But we can't always leave our bodies behind in either of these two ways. We experience and interact with the world through our bodies, and at times they assert their presence. Our bodies are often more present to our consideration when there's a problem with them or as we age. They tire, get sick or injured, and fail to sustain our lives. At these moments, our bodies impinge on our attention and demand that we think about the vulnerability they bring. In her book *Illness: The Cry of the Flesh*, Havi Carel writes that "the healthy body is transparent, taken for granted. . . . It is only when something goes wrong with the body that we begin to notice it" (Carel 2019, 33). In such moments, our body's vulnerability becomes obvious. As sociologist and bioethicist Tom Shakespeare notes, "to be born [human] is to be vulnerable, to fall prey to disease and pain and suffering, and ultimately to die" (Shakespeare 2014, 109). Our embodiment is a living reminder of our dependence and finitude.

At yet other times, we give a lot of consideration to our or others' bodies. But often when we do this, we idealize these bodies, rendering them less "messy" or "complex" than they really are. All too frequently, reflection on the body assumes, even if implicitly, an idealization that obscures important facts about what it means for humans to be "enfleshed." David Linton, for instance, writes about "the menstral masquerade," a set of social pressures for women to "hide the physical evidence of one's cycle" (Linton 2013, 58) despite the fact that most post-puberty, pre-menopausal females menstruate. Even though roughly half of the human population will menstruate at some point in their lives, there is considerable pressure not to engage with this fact. Menstruation is an example of what Clare Chambers calls "shametenance" – issues where we "maintain shame by actively shaming others, or simply by keeping things private, silent, invisible, unsayable" (Chambers 2022, 70). Menstruation isn't unique in this way. There is a wide range of facts about our messy bodies that we're taught from an early age that it's not appropriate to discuss in public. The social pressure to make our bodies look a certain way or to keep certain bodily processes hidden is significant.

Our idealizations of the body can be problematic. As discussed in greater detail later, the range of what our cultural ethos says human bodies *should* be like is much narrower than the range of what human bodies actually *are* like. Bodies deemed aesthetically pleasing are treated better than bodies that are not. Bodies that can accomplish various fairly arbitrary even if impressive feats are given large cultural esteem and economic influence. (Think of professional sports.) Disabled, misshapen, or scarred bodies are stigmatized, hidden from view, and treated as if they have less moral value. Social pressures encourage us to pretend that we're less dependent on others than we are.

These idealized understandings do not properly reflect the full range of human experience. But this is not only a problem for how we think about bodies. As a wide range of scholars of disability, race, and feminist thought have pointed out, the ways that culture singles out certain sorts of bodies as nonideal reinforce a range of problematic social norms. In the United States, black and brown bodies, for instance, are often assumed to be more dangerous, resulting in increased levels of police force, much of it lethal. How women's bodies look impacts how they're treated, from cat-calling to cultural preoccupation with thinness. Visibly disabled bodies tend to fair less well in job hunting even if their disability is unrelated to the nature of the job.

Taking the full range of human experience seriously requires that we think carefully about human embodiment, the fact that we have bodies that impact our experiences in the world. We are born, live, and die as embodied beings. For those religious traditions that include belief in the resurrection, that too is embodied. This Element is an attempt to encourage serious thinking about a range of issues related to embodiment. More specifically, this Element explores a number of ways that reflection on bodies in their concrete particularities is important for philosophical and religious thought. It begins with a consideration of why certain forms of embodiment are often believed to be problematic. It then explores how a number of features of bodies, most notably facts about disabilities and other stigmatized forms of embodiment, can reveal important truths about human nature, embodiment, and dependence.

1.2 Us and Our Bodies

Thinking about fundamental human dependence in the context of philosophical and religious reflection on embodiment, especially in a text of this size, requires making a number of decisions. Comprehensiveness has to be sacrificed for brevity. For one, I shall engage exclusively with "Western" philosophical positions, though I draw on a wide range of methodological approaches. In terms of theological context, the treatment here will assume Christianity. In one sense, this is unfortunate since too much contemporary philosophy of religion has been restricted to philosophy of Christianity. (For a discussion of this problem, see Mizrahi 2019 and Simmons 2019.) Philosophy of religion should be diversified as a discipline in terms of which religions it engages. But there are two reasons for focusing attention on Christianity in this Element. First, it is the religious tradition that I know the best. (I didn't say it was a particularly *good* philosophical reason, but expertise does matter for careful engagement.) Second, Christian belief in the bodily resurrection of the dead and the incarnation offer unique doctrines from which to consider issues of embodiment. While some branches of Judaism also believe in the resurrection, "it is almost always left vague as to what sort of a body the resurrected will possess" (Wright 2008, 43). Christian philosophers and theologians have given the matter significant thought.

There are, of course, philosophical and religious traditions that don't think our bodies are fundamentally part of us. Instead, for these traditions, what we are most fundamentally is an immaterial mind or soul. While our mind or soul might happen to interact with a body, the body is not an essential part of who we are. For instance, in his dialogue the *Phaedo*, Plato recounts a conversation between his teacher Socrates and Simmias. Socrates indicates that despite being sentenced to death by Athens for corrupting the youth, he doesn't fear death since he hopes that it will bring him some future good. Death, says Socrates, is nothing more than "the separation of the soul from the body" (*Phaedo*, 64c). When we die and our soul is no longer connected to a physical body, we will better be able to come to knowledge:

> The body keeps us busy in a thousand ways because of its need for nurture. Moreover, if certain diseases befall it, they impede our search for the truth. It [the body] fills us with wants, desires, fears, all sorts of illusions and much nonsense, so that, as it is said, in truth and in fact no thought of any kind ever comes to us from the body. . . . If we are ever able to have pure knowledge, we must escape from the body and observe things in themselves with the soul by itself. (*Phaedo*, 66b-2)

Because bodily death should not be feared but anticipated in this way, Socrates thinks of philosophy as "practice for dying and death" (*Phaedo*, 64a).

Similarly, seventeenth-century French philosopher Reneé Descartes is well-known for his own dualism. Like Socrates, Descartes thinks that the soul does not die when the body dies. The soul, he thinks, is immortal. For Descartes, the soul is "nothing but a thinking thing; that is, a mind, or intellect, or understanding, or reason" (*Meditations on First Philosophy*, med. 2). The soul is not physical, only a thinking thing, and it interacts with the body, which is physical but does no thinking. The mind and the body are "wholly diverse" (*Meditations on First Philosophy*, med. 6).

The focus on the "mind" or "soul" at the expense of the body in Western philosophy isn't limited to just these two paradigmatic instances. The dualistic tradition is much more robust than has been canvased here. Reflecting on the history of philosophy, Drew Leder finds that "within the Western philosophical tradition the body has often been regarded as a force of negativity, an obstacle to the soul's attempt to secure knowledge, virtue, or eternal life. . . . A certain devaluing of the body, either in the form of neglect, deprecation, or outright condemnation, has formed an ongoing theme in our intellectual history" (Leder 1990, 127). But not all bodies are the same, and the devaluation of the body in general is compatible with devaluating some kinds of bodies more than others. Joel Michael Reynolds notes the same phenomenon: "the life of the body for the 'Western canon' [in philosophy] is so often held to be worth less than that of the mind – and the lives of certain bodies and certain minds deemed worth less still" (Reynolds 2022, 1). Feminist philosophers, philosophers of disability, and philosophers of race have noted how the focus on the "mind" over the body has tended to devalue women, disabled people, and racial minorities. Feminist historians have shown that the justification of women's oppression often includes claims that women's bodily emotions overwhelm their "reason," associated with the mind. Treating women differently, it has been claimed, is not only a way of keeping their bodies under control but also actually a way of caring for them given how their particularly embodiment works. Here we note that claims about particular kinds of embodiment often serve oppressive social systems (see Meynell 2009 and Glenn 2010 for discussions).

Historically, Christianity has not been immune from these dualistic ways of thinking. (This, in one sense, should be obvious since Descartes was himself Catholic.) The Early Church wrestled with gnosticism. A nebulous set of beliefs both within and without the Church, gnosticism understood the body as evil or a prison. Gnosticism strives for redemption understood as liberation from creation through the discovery of secret knowledge or *gnosis* that would free the divine spirit from the body and the material world at large. Largely due to the influence of Irenaeus and Tertullian, both Church fathers, Christian orthodoxy would come to reject gnosticism. While one can find forms of nongnostic dualism regarding human nature throughout Church history, Caroline Walker Bynum's work shows that the majority of the tradition has held that humans are a "psychosomatic unity" of body and soul (Bynum 1995).

Coupling the early credal assertion that God is "creator of heaven and earth" with the Scriptural declaration that upon creating "God saw that it was good," the Church affirmed the goodness of the physical world. Rejecting the goodness of the any part of the physical world, including the physical body, runs afoul of the Christian commitment to the fundamental goodness of all of creation.

Contemporary theologian N. T. Wright unpacks the implications of this in a number of his books. A central thrust of some of his work emphasizes that God's kingdom is not what we escape to when we die, as many contemporary Christians seem to assume. Thinking that the Christian life is primarily about escaping the physical world for a future spiritual realm, according to Wright, is rooting in "the residual Platonism that has infected whole swaths of Christian thinking and has misled people into supporting that Christians are meant to devalue the present world and our present bodies" (Wright 2008, 18). Our bodies are part of the "living sacrifice" that Christians are called to make to God as part of proper our worship (Romans 12:1). Taking physicality seriously rather than hoping to escape it one day gives us reason to value the body, and the rest of the physical world, now. More recently, his *History and Eschatology* argues that misunderstanding the history of the present physical world contributes to a misunderstanding of eschatology. Here Wright argues that the influence of Platonic dualism has led to "modern Western Christianity abandon[ing] the biblical hope of new creation and bodily resurrection" (Wright 2019, 33) in favor of a gnostic escapism. (We'll return to eschatological bodies in Section 2.)

Christian theology, as Wright understands it however, rejects the attempt to escape either the body or the present world. Instead, for Christianity "new creation means new *creation*, the *renewal* of the present world rather than its abandonment and replacement by some other kind of world altogether" (Wright 2017, 2). For Wright, the original creation is included within, though transcended by, God's eschatological purposes in the new creation. A central claim of Wright's earlier *Surprised by Hope* is the claim that the Christian theological virtue of hope is in redemption not escapism; a renewal of creation rather than an abandonment of it. Wright describes 1 Corinthians 15 as a theology of new creation rather than an abandonment of creation. The coming Kingdom of God "refers not to our escape from this world into another one, but to God's sovereign rule coming 'on earth as it is in heaven'" (Wright 2008, 18).

The goodness of creation is also reaffirmed in Christ's incarnation and bodily resurrection. In hypostatically uniting with a human body in the Incarnation, the Second Person of the Trinity became fully human, including in terms of embodiment. And yet this could not have happened if having a body were in some way bad since the Incarnate Christ is also fully divine, having all of the divine perfections. In Christ, the goodness of embodied human existence is affirmed. Cole Arthur Riley notes that "when we neglect the physical, it inevitably suffocates the image of a God who ate, slept, cried, bled, grew, and healed" (Riley 2022, 60). It's not just embodiment in the abstract that is good; having a *particular* body with all its specificity is good. Furthermore, Christ's bodily resurrection and ascension into heaven serves as a signpost of anticipated future cosmic redemption. What is affirmed as good isn't just those bodies that meet some idealization that rules out certain forms of embodiment a priori. The resurrected Christ had scars, some of which were big enough to stick one's hand into (John 20:27). An approach to the afterlife that undercuts the importance of the body, including the resurrected body, for being human is at odds with the historical Christian faith.

A central thrust of Christina Van Dyke's recent *A Hidden Wisdom* is to show "how prejudices against women, emotions, and the body have played a significant role" (Van Dyke 2022, 4) in shaping philosophical and theological attention in parts of the Christian tradition. In particular, the overly narrow approach to what counts as a mystical tradition has led to a "dismissal and/or mistrust of female reports of embodied mystical experiences" (Van Dyke 2022, 8). For female mystics like Julian of Norwich, "knowing ourselves as bodily subjects . . . becomes a way of knowing Christ, who is simultaneously fully human and fully divine. . . . Christ's incarnation occurs at least in part as an effort to connect our flesh-and-blood humanity more closely to God's divinity" (Van Dyke 2022, 59 and 106). The resurrection body will be physical, but will be transformed much like Christ's was.

1.3 Bodies and Imagination

Another way we idealize the body is by thinking they're more disconnected from the social world than they are. It's true that many of the facts about a person's body are independent of what they or anyone else thinks about their body. Nevertheless, we engage bodily with the world, and other people engage with us in light of our bodies and how they understand or interpret them. For instance, others' reactions to us and valuation of us depends on how they value or devalue our bodies. Many daily reactions remind us that our culture values and valorizes some kinds of bodies over others. There is a boundary, though an admittedly fuzzy and changing one, between bodies that are deemed culturally acceptable and those that aren't. And this boundary connects with our normative evaluation of the value of the people whose bodies they are and the kinds of lives that are worth living.

One reason it's important to take seriously the full range of human embodiment is because our common assumptions shape our collective imagination. Consider the beginning of David Foster Wallace's well-known *This Is Water*, originally given as the commitment address at Kenyon College in 2007. Wallace begins with the following parable:

> There are these two young fish swimming along and they happen to meet an older fish swimming the other way, who nods at them and says "Morning, boys. How's the water?" And the two young fish swim on for a bit, and then eventually one of them looks over at the other and goes "What the hell is water?"
>
> This is a standard requirement of US commencement speeches, the deployment of didactic little parable-ish stories. The story thing turns out to be one of the better, less bullshitty conventions of the genre. . . . But if you're worried that I plan to present myself here as the wise, older fish explaining what water is to you younger fish, please don't be. I am not the wise old fish. The point of the fish story is merely that the most obvious, important realities are often the ones that are hardest to see and talk about. (Wallace 2009, 3–8)

Part of our cultural "water" is the assumption of what Robert McRuer calls "compulsory able-bodiedness." By this, McRuer means that able-bodiedness "masquerades as a nonidentity, as the natural order of things" (McRuer 2006, 1). We often fail to notice the importance of our assumptions about what bodies should be like precisely because of how prevalent these assumptions are. As a result, those whose bodies are not disabled often don't even notice the ways our lives are shaped by this assumption of compulsory able-bodiedness. Environments, both physical and social, are built for certain individuals. Architecture and public access default to a narrow range of what kinds of bodies need to be given consideration, which in turn puts additional demands on others. Philosopher S. Kay Toombs wrote about how sick bodies, like her own, are forced to confront environments not built with them in mind:

> With respect to the changed character of a physical space, it is important to recognize that those of us who negotiate space in a wheelchair live in a world that is in many respects designed for those who can stand upright. Until recently all of our architecture and every avenue of public access was designed for those with working legs. Hence, people with disabilities (and those who regularly accompany them) necessarily come to view the world through the medium of the limits and possibilities of their own bodies. One is always "sizing up" the environment to see whether it is accommodating for the changed body. (Toombs 2001, 250).

In this context, disability scholar Joseph Stramondo talks about "the imaginative failure" many nondisabled people experience when thinking about living with a disability. Nondisabled people often can't imagine how normal a life with a disability is for those who have them. The unimaginable nature of someone else's life doesn't mean their life is automatically worse than ours. Disabled lives can have just as much well-being as lives without disabilities (Campbell and Stramondo 2017). Bryce Huebner similarly notes that our "embodied trajectories through socially structured space will impact what we think and what we see as a possibility" (Huebner 2016). That is to say, our embodiment shapes our experience. It used to be fairly common for parents of children with Down syndrome to seek plastic surgery to make them look more "normal." While this surgery was purely cosmetic rather than functional, it was motivated by the desire to secure social goods for their children that visibly disabled individuals often don't have easy access to given cultural expectations.

If we don't notice how significantly our lives are structured by compulsory able-bodiedness, we also might not notice how much we assume that others' experiences need to be like ours to be equally valuable. This often leads us to think, for instance, that embodied lives with autism or other disabilities are less worth living. But this isn't the case. Autistic author and neurodiversity advocate Daniel Bowman Jr. encourages nondisabled people to take seriously the experiences of autistics and other disabled people without devaluing those lives or experiences: "you're learning about what it means to be human" (Bowman Jr. 2021, 35).

The point about disabled bodies generalizes to other kinds of bodies as well. How we think about embodiment reflects what we individually care about. We often shape our bodies, through exercise or fashion or tattoos and other body art, to present our preferences or values. We find others attractive because of features of their bodies. Lookism refers to the prejudice people can have toward others because of facts about how attractive their bodies are interpreted to be. But it's not enough to look only at individual reactions to particular bodies. There are deep cultural pressures which result in significant differences in how people are treated by social institutions. For instance, those who are black or trans or fat run additional risk to their safety in public. Sometimes these additional risks come with the support of larger social structures such as the police or the medical establishment. Think of the need for the Black Lives Matter Movement. Or think of the Tuskegee syphilis experiment, the forcible relocation of Japanese Americans during World War II, the abuse endured by disabled people in state-run institutions like Willowbrook. All of these are instances of social injustices performed against a group of people because of their bodies. And even in cases that don't involve social injustices, social expectations about bodies shape how we live our lives. There is pressure to modify our bodies to make them more appealing or acceptable to others, which Clare Chambers chronicles at length in her work (Chambers 2022).

It's also worth noting the ways that contemporary society valorizes productivity but doesn't like to admit how our bodies place limits on that productivity. Bodies need rest, for instance. And the ways our bodies work isn't fully up to us, defying our attempts to bend them to our wills: As Susan Wendell puts it: "Refusal to come to terms with the full reality of bodily life, including those aspects of it that are rejected culturally [such as disability], leads people to embrace the myth of control, whose essence is the belief that it is possible by means of human action, to have the bodies we want and to avoid illness, disability, and death" (Wendell 1996, 9).

The norms we expect bodies to measure up to are deeply culturally shaped. Thinking carefully about embodiment requires that we "take into account the intersections of body, experience, and culture" (Connolly 2001, 182.) The expectations that we hold our bodies to, as well as the idealizations that we make regarding how we think about our bodies, are deeply socially constructed. Sometimes we feel the pressure of these norms when our views about our own bodies conflict with them. But it's also the case that what we ourselves think about bodies, including our own, and their importance are greatly shaped by larger cultural views and pressures. Women, for instance, can feel the pressure to wear make-up and spend considerable time and money making their bodies look a certain way even while acknowledging how these pressures come from patriarchy. How others treat our bodies shapes our self-understanding. Sometimes we don't even recognize the extent to which our own beliefs and values are shaped by these social forces. Wendell continues that "the disciplines of normality like those of femininity are not only enforced by others but internalized. For many of us our proximity to the standards of normality is an important aspect of our identity and our sense of social acceptability an aspect of our self-respect" (Wendell 1996, 88).

Much of our dissatisfaction with ourselves or with others may seem to be located in our bodies. However, careful reflection shows that this dissatisfaction isn't primarily in our bodies but rather rooted in the lived experience of how our bodies are understood in the social environment. The assumptions that others in our social communities make about our bodies shape our experiences. Bodies that differ from what others expect are singled out for abuse or mistreatment. For example, the most common basis for bullying among children is weight. Or, to consider another example, many nondisabled persons will describe a wheelchair user as being "wheelchair bound," often not noticing the negative valence of such phrasing. However, wheelchair users experience their wheelchairs as extensions of their bodies or as tools for liberation, particularly in environments that would otherwise be inaccessible to them.

As argued throughout this section, people whose bodies are deemed to be nonstandard in some way can come to internalize the larger cultural expectations, even if they are disadvantaged by them. Research shows that media reinforcement of idealized beauty standards and equation of body size with health contributes to body dissatisfaction, lower self-image, and internalization of the "thin ideal" and significant negative health implications (Mills et al. 2017). Such evaluations of bodies, by both the self and others, have consequences. Obesity stigma has been found to influence jurors' evaluations of defendants (Flint 2015) and health care treatment (Amy, Aalborg, Lyons, and Keranen 2006). But researchers have shown that BMI (body mass index) as the standard metric for determining obesity is extremely problematic as an indicator of ill health (Reiheld 2015). In fact, some researchers now think that weight stigma itself "poses a threat to health" (Tomiyama et al. 2018, 6) that is greater than that from fat bodies themselves. Our social systems – health care, education, employment, and so on – function within larger webs of pressures and exceptions of what bodies should be like. Those in power and aligned with the such systems to a large degree dictate how bodies are understood. These assumptions about bodies don't have to be conscious or intentional to shape our experiences. But we'll be better positioned if we reflect more explicitly on what our embodiment can tell us about the human condition.

1.4 The Plan

The plan for the rest of this Element is as follows. Section 2 explores in greater detail disabilities, and how disabled bodies are often the focus for various misconceptions about the human condition. These misconceptions reveal how strong the assumptions about what makes certain forms of embodiment "good" are. I expand this discussion, in Section 3, to include other kinds of embodiment that are often seen as problematic. Section 4 draws on embodiment to investigate human dependence in a number of forms: dependence on our physical environments, on others, and on God. The Element concludes in Section 5 with a discussion of some of the ethical consequences that result from our embodiment and the dependence that it reveals.

2 Dispelling Some Misconceptions

2.1 Conceptual Frames

The previous section raised the issue of what Drew Leder calls "the corporeal absence," which tends to happen either when our embodiment disappears from our attention or when we engage in idealization about what our embodiment involves. These two tendencies are not unrelated. When certain bodies are considered "standard" or paradigmatic instances of what human bodies should be like, it is easier for them to escape our notice. Our eyes don't linger on an eighteen-month old being spoon-fed by a parent when we're eating at the neighborhood gastropub. But if a body doesn't live up to our cultural expectations, suddenly their presence captures our notice. If it's instead a teenage child being spoon-fed by a parent because they have motor control difficulties due to a genetic condition or if they drool or their muscle control is marked by spastic wiggling, their embodiment quickly attracts attention from neighboring tables. Since teenage bodies "aren't *supposed to be like that*," their particular embodiment no longer escapes notice.

How we think about bodies, and what we expect them to be like, is part of what sociologists call "a conceptual frame." A conceptual frame is the general schema within which an issue is approached, which also shapes how we conceptualized other related ideas. Various frames not only shape how we think about a situation but also make it harder for us to be open to alternate ways of understanding and evaluating the same issue. The stronger a conceptual frame is, the more difficult it is to dislodge. This is especially true given that conceptual frames are social, reinforced by the frames of those around us. For instance, one conceptual frame is that "thin is good." Within this frame, larger corpulent bodies are taken to be unhealthy, unwell, or risky. This makes it more difficult for us to think that such bodies can be healthy or good (Saguy 2013). And because of the ubiquity of this frame, we make assumptions about people that are often problematic. Fat people, for instance, report having their health concerns downplayed by doctors who urge them to "lose the weight" to feel better, even if there is no evidence connecting their weight to their medical concern. The frame then comes to have normative implications for how we think about people according to that frame. If "thin is good," then fat bodies are conceptualized as "bad" in some way. Another conceptual frame regarding embodiment found in much contemporary Western film or literature is that whiteness is the default race, so much that it "seems not to be there as a subject at all" (Fessenden 1999, 23), while other racialized bodies are taken to be exceptions. This framing, Fessenden continues, "makes it hard not only to analyze whiteness but even hard to see it, much less to see its meanings as socially produced" (Fessenden 1999, 23).

There are lots of conceptual frames regarding embodiment. Many of them, much like "thin is good," are problematic. The primary purpose of this section is to dispel a few such misconceptions of how we often think about embodiment, even if only implicitly. Some of these misconceptions are assumptions that we pick up from our cultural contexts and the cognitive frames embedded in them. But once these assumptions are brought to light and made explicit, it becomes easier for us to recognize why they are problematic. We'll also note that many of these misconceptions have contributed to mistreatment of those individuals who fail to live up to those cultural assumptions about what bodies "ought to be like." This section focuses primarily on a number of conceptual frames regarding disability that misconstrue the human experience. This focus is meant to only be illustrative, not exhaustive. While disability is only one kind of embodiment that is devalued, the general points from this section can also generalize to other conceptual frames regarding embodiment as well. But since, as Rosemarie Garland Thomson puts it, "disability, perhaps more than other [bodily] differences, demands a reckoning with the messiness of bodily variety" (Thomson 1997, 23), it is an especially good place to start.

2.2 The "Disability Is Bad" Frame

One of the most prevalent conceptual frames about disability is that "disability is bad"; that is, having a disability automatically makes a person worse off simply in virtue of having that disability. This conceptual frame has a long history in Western cultures. Numerous Western cultures have historically had infanticide as a common response to disabled infants, often through death by exposure. Aristotle in the *Politics* suggests that legislators should enact "a law that no *deformed* child shall live, but that on the ground of an *excess* in the number of children" (*Politics*, 1335b20-22). Recently, some scholars have challenged this view, claiming that the attribution of widespread death by exposure in history isn't supported by the available evidence (Scott 2001).

Similarly, Metzler has called into question the view that in the West "ancient or medieval societies *invariably* saw a link between sin and illness [that] appears to be the dominant historiographical notion on the subject of disability" (Metzler 2005, 13). Caution is thus needed lest we make too sweeping of claims about a single historical approach to disability, even if just in the West. But on the whole many scholars think that "significant forces in the modern world have contributed to the view that individuals with disabilities are of less value than those who are not disabled" (Gaudet 2017, 46).

The "disability is bad" frame can easily be found even apart from disability being a justification for infanticide. There is a common assumption that having a disability automatically negatively impacts a person's well-being (see Campbell and Stramondo 2017). In the excellent collection of advice from autistic adults *Sincerely, Your Autistic Child*, autistic disability rights advocate Heidi Wangelin imagines a conversation she wishes she could have with her younger self. Wangelin gives this piece of advice to her earlier self by saying, "I would reassure her that she's going to be just fine. She's not broken, just different – a good kind of different" (Wangelin 2021, 45).

What Wangelin here illustrates is two ways of thinking about the impact of disabilities on a person's well-being, the difference between what Elizabeth Barnes calls "bad-difference" views of disability and "mere-difference" views. The central thrust of Barnes' book *The Minority Body* is to argue for a mere-difference view. Barnes' book is explicit that she's only focusing on physical disabilities, not disabilities in general. Nevertheless, we can apply her distinction to different ways of thinking about disability more broadly. The "rough and ready" distinction between the two families of views is as follows. Those views which hold that "disability is by itself something that makes you worse off [are] 'bad-difference' views of disability" (Barnes 2016, 55). In contrast, mere-difference views are those according to which having a disability doesn't by itself or automatically make you worse off. The "disability is bad" frame often leads to the unargued-for assumption that disability always involves bad-difference.

Evidence of the "disability is bad" frame is also found in ableism. The discipline of disability studies argues that the lived experiences of disabled people aren't best understood as a natural, unmediated result of their bodies' conditions. Rather, disability studies "theorizes disability as an important social category whose contingent meanings are forged, negotiated, and transformed with a cauldron of lived experience and relationship, conceptual and built architectures, normalizing ideologies, and the globalized uneven distribution of life chances" (Hall et al. 2017, 405). Much of the badness that comes from disability, then, isn't a direct result of the bodily condition itself but how that bodily condition is treated.

Ableism is a kind of disability prejudice, akin to how racism and sexism are prejudice based on racial and sexed categories. Different scholars describe ableism in a number of overlapping ways:

> "the oppression of disabled people" in which a person "starts to be stigmatized as 'different'" (House 1981, 34; this *may* be the first usage of the term in the literature)
>
> ideas, practices, institutions, and social relations that presumed able-bodiedness (Chouinard 1997, 380)
>
> the devaluation of disability (Hehir 2002, 2)
>
> a set of assumptions (conscious or unconscious) and practices that promote the differential or unequal treatment of people because of actual or presumed disabilities (Kumari Campbell 2009, 4)
>
> a system that places value on people's bodies and minds based on societally constructed ideas of normalcy, intelligence, excellence and productivity. . . . This form of systemic oppression leads to people and society determining who is valuable and worthy based on a person's appearance and/or their ability to satisfactorily produce, excel and "behave." (Lewis 2020)

Sometimes ableism, much like racism and sexism, is thought to be only a function of individual attitudes or treatment. However, all three are best understood as at least partly structural. When, as some of these descriptions capture, ableism becomes enshrined in social systems, it can lead to oppression. Feminist philosopher Marilyn Frye argues that oppression happens when a system constrains the relevant options for individuals, restricting what they can do given those social forces:

> The experience of oppressed people is that the living of one's life is confined and shaped by forces and barriers which are not accidental or occasional and hence avoidable, but are systematically related to each other in such a way as to catch one between and among them and restrict or penalize motion in any direction. It is the experience of being caged in: all avenues, in every direction, are blocked or booby trapped. (Frye 1983, 4)

Frye illustrates oppressive systems using the metaphor of a birdcage: When examined individually, no single wire prevents the bird in a cage from flying away. It is only when one steps back and takes a macroscopic view of the wires and the relationships between them *as a whole* that one realizes that they form "a network of systematically related barriers" (Frye 1983, 5). Oppression is, on her view, a macroscopic phenomenon:

> It is now possible to grasp one of the reasons why oppression can be hard to see and recognize: one can study the elements of an oppressive structure with great care and some good will without seeing the structure as a whole, and hence without seeing or being able to understand that one is looking at a cage and that there are people there who are caged, whose motion and mobility are restricted, whose lives are shaped and reduced. (Frye 1983, 5)

While all of us face limitations and frustrations, only those who in virtue of their membership in some group or category are subject to social structures who enclose and reduce their options as a whole are oppressed. Significant scholarship has shown the results of the history of oppression of disabled people because of compulsory able-bodiedness and ableism (see, for instance, Shapiro 1994, Baynton 2001, Solomon 2012, especially chapters 2–5 and 7, and McGuire 2016). While disability-based oppression may not be as severe and widespread as it used to be, it has not been eradicated. Such oppression both grows out of and reinforces ableism.

2.3 Christianity, Disability, and Embodiment

As with other theological issues, referring to "the Christian tradition" as if it were a single unified whole is overly simplistic. Christian reflection on and care for disabled bodies is both complicated and diverse. Many Christians throughout Church history have evidenced profound care for disabled people, individually as well as communally. Furthermore, as David T. Mitchell notes, talking about the history of disability is complex because "disability has refused to remain linguistically stable, in-and-of-itself," a fact that "demonstrates the variables of the body and its socially generated interpretations" (Mitchell 1999, ix). That is, in many ways "disability" is a modern concept that we read back into history to characterize a wide range of bodily states that historically may or may not have been understood earlier as disabling. One of the best discussions of the historical factors that have shaped how what is now referred to as disability has be understood over time is Henri-Jacques Stiker's *Corps infirmes et sociétés*, translated into English as *A History of Disability* (Stiker 2000). According to Stiker, "the dividing line [between being disabled and not being disabled] is not always sharp, even from an objective point of view. Mental and social categories of defect and disease [and disability] have varied, we admit, but however the boundary is drawn in various periods and societies there is always a distinction" (Stiker 2000, 9) between those forms of embodiment that are taken to be acceptable or normal and those that are not. What is understood to be a disability is historically situated and contingent, shaped by how various institutions seek and wield power (see also Tremain 2017).

At the same time, as with other kinds of exclusion and problematic treatment of marginalized groups, there is also a well-documented history of embodied conditions that we'd now describe as involving disability being othered or marginalized in religious history. Under the Jewish law, for instance, many disabilities were considered ritually unclean, resulting in exclusion due to concerns about purity and sanctity. Physically disabled individuals are prohibited from being priests in Leviticus 21 due to being "defective." Disabled bodies were seen as a contagion that needed to be protected against.

While this is the religious context that he inherited, Jesus sought to break the association between disability and individual or familial fault. In the Gospel of John, Jesus encounters a man born blind. His disciples ask in a way that is illustrative of their religious understanding: "Rabbi, who sinned, this man or his parents, that he was born blind?" (John 9:2, ESV). Jesus denies either's sin caused the man's blindness, instead healing him so that he could find welcome into the community that had previously excluded him. Jesus then "calls his disciples to work on behalf of those pushed to the margins socially, religiously, and economically" (Clark-Soles 2017, 351). This attempt to undermine the link between disability and sin is, however, tempered by other parts of the New Testament which fail to take a stance critical of the "disability is bad" frame. Paul repeatedly uses disabling conditions such as blindness as his primary metaphors for sin. Commenting on the New Testament, Biblical scholar Sarah Melcher writes that "people with disability are implicitly or explicitly cast out of the kingdom of God" (Melcher 2017, 21) despite Jesus' teachings.

While he's commenting specifically on how disability was understood in medieval Christian Europe, Joshua R. Eyler's comments can also be understood to apply more broadly to the Christian tradition as a whole: "While it is certainly accurate to say that *some* people in the Middle Ages believed disability to be God's punishment for sin, this way of understanding medieval disability has only a limited viability. In truth, there are many lenses through which medieval societies viewed disability" (Eyler 2010, 3). Eyler, similar to Metzler's work mentioned on page 14, is correct about the nonuniformity of a single lens or frame through which disabled have been understood and evaluated historically. Even if there is a lack of uniformity, it still remains the case that significant swaths of the Western and Christian traditions have viewed disability through the "disability is bad" frame. (While much of this discussion focuses on what is now often referred to as "physical disability" as opposed to other sorts disabilities, note that these other categories of disability also have to do with embodiment. Intellectual disability is rooted in brain physiology, and can be caused by bodily trauma such as a traumatic brain injury. Increasing evidence points to autism as at least partially caused by genetic and epigenetic factors.) Physical disability was linked, even if not perfectly, with monstrosity and dangerousness. Even when the response to physical disability changed after the United State's Civil War and World War I from isolation and institutionalization to one of rehabilitation, the framing was still there to eliminate or at least minimize the impact of disability and return the person to as "normal" (that is, nondisabled) as possible (Stiker 2000, chapter 5). And research suggests that such negative views of disability are actually more common among American Christians than among the American population as a whole (see Timpe 2018, chapter 5).

2.4 Resurrection Misconceptions

James Baldwin was an American author and activist against both racial and sexual oppression. In his 1963 collection *The Fire Next Time*, Baldwin talks about the segregation he experienced in Christian churches in the United States. He notes that the segregation found in churches and the wider culture can come to shape our eschatological vision: "the vision people hold of the world to come is but a reflection, with predictable wishful distortions, of the world in which they live" (Balwin 1992, 40). In a parallel way, the conceptual frame that "disability is bad" can also shape how we think about the nature of bodies in our eschatological vision.

Details of eschatology are part of speculative theology, and so what is said must be held tentatively. In the Apostles' Creed, Christianity affirms "the resurrection of the physical body and the life everlasting," but beyond that few details are settled by Christian orthodoxy. One way to begin thinking about resurrection bodies is in light of Jesus' own resurrected body, which according to Christian scriptures and tradition bore scars from the crucifixion, including a wound on Jesus' side from the spear big enough for the apostle Thomas to put his hand inside (John 20:27). Numerous philosophers and theologians have noted that this has implications for how we should think about resurrected bodies in general. In commenting on the bodily resurrection and assumption of Jesus, Christina Van Dyke notes that according to Christian theology, "Christ did not just *become* human; Christ *remains* human, and Christ's ascension into heaven was bodily as well as spiritual, assuring us that our immortal existence will not be that of disembodied angels but that of flesh and blood creatures – albeit flesh and blood that have been transformed into incorruptibility" (Van Dyke 2022, 190). His resurrection is both a promise and a model for the resurrection of the dead in general. Regarding Jesus' resurrection embodiment, Kate Bowen-Evans writes, "the scars on Jesus' own resurrected body indicate something of this eschatological understanding; the disabilities of life do not indicate a flawed life but a bodily life common to all, including Jesus" (Bowen-Evans

2022, 173). For Bowen-Evans, recognizing this has implication beyond just disability. Such a "disability hermeneutic has a liberating effect for more than just those labeled disabled, but provides affirmation for anyone whose body is considered weak or inferior, disabled or deviant in their society. Each marginalized believer, of any bodily situation, is given the manifestation of the spirit for the common good" (Bowen-Evans 2022, 174).

There isn't a consensus as to the nature of human eschatological existence. Some endorse annihilationism, according to which the damned will cease to exist. At least in practice, some lay Christians talk as if people will become disembodied spirits or angels in the afterlife. However, the dominant Christian view is bodily resurrection not only for those in heaven, the redeemed, but also for those in hell, the damned. As Van Dyke puts it, this dominant understanding holds that "the afterlife includes expectations not only for individual conscious experience but for individual *embodied* experiences" (Van Dyke 2022, 190). The thirteenth-century Italian poet Dante Alighieri, in his influential *Divine Comedy*, described the souls in purgatory as disembodied, which is why the souls there purging their remaining sin were surprised that Dante, still embodied, cast a shadow. But upon perfecting their character and being "perfect, pure, and ready for the Stars" (*Purgatorio* canto XXXIII line 146), they would be physically resurrected before entering into heaven.

It is common for folks to assume, on the basis of the "disability is bad" frame or by equating disability with disease or suffering, that disability has no place in the eschaton. Amy Kenny's book *My Body Is Not a Prayer Request* contains many stories of other people, including complete strangers, suggesting that God's plan is to heal her of her disability. Kenny begins the book by recounting an encounter with a woman, a stranger, who says "God told me to pray for you. . . . God wants to heal you" (Kenny 2022, 1). Kenny notes that the woman's assumption that because Kenny uses a cane she needs to be cured "ropes God into her ableism" (Kenny 2022, 1). So much of this well-being but misguided theological reflection on disability reads like Job's friends' response to his predicament: seeking to find a way to blame Job rather than questioning the friends' undying assumption. The lack of healing is either blamed on Kenny's lack of faith or shifts to an eschatological promise. People "avoid the discomfort of messy lived experience by constantly promising a completeness yet to come. 'You'll be whole one day' or 'you'll be running in heaven,' they promise through pursed lips, as though I am not yet already a new creation" (Kenny 2022, 27).

Similarly John Swinton, Harriet Mowat, and Susannah Baines tell the story of Ian, an adult with Down syndrome, who had recently died:

> Ian had been taken to the mortuary and laid out. When the care worker had gone to see Ian's body, he noticed that there was absolutely no sign of Down syndrome! Even the telltale lines on his hands had (apparently miraculously) disappeared. The caretaker spoke to the undertaker who did not know that Ian had Down syndrome. Others noticed this. One person was spooked. The caretaker put it this way: "Where Ian is, he'll not have Down syndrome because he'll have a resurrection body." (Swinton et al. 2011, 8)

This sentiment that people like Ian will need to be resurrected with "cured" or "fixed" bodies has precedent among the Doctors of the Church. Augustine, for instance, held that "we are not justified in affirming even of monstrosities . . . that they shall rise again in their deformity, and not rather with an amended and perfected body" (*Enchiridion*, chapter 87, "The Case for Monstrous Births"). Medieval theologian Thomas Aquinas writes in his *Summa Theologiae* that "blindness and lameness are kinds of sickness" (*ST* IIa.IIae q. 32 a. 2, ad 2). Aquinas is explicit that Christ's resurrection body will retain marks of his crucifixion. He attributes to Bede, a seventh-century historian and doctor of the Church, the view that Christ's resurrection body had scars "to wear them as an everlasting trophy of His victory," adding that "although those openings of the wounds break the continuity of the tissue, still the greater beauty of the glory compensates for all this, so that the body is not less entire, but more perfected" (*ST* III q. 54 a. 4, *respondio* and ad 1). But when considering resurrection bodies in general, Aquinas described the resurrected body as having four attributes, as was common for medieval theologians: *impassibility*, *sublety*, *agility*, and *clarity*. (See Van Van Dyke 2020 for a further discussion of these attributes in the resurrected body in the medieval tradition.) Each body will appear as "if there has been no error in the working of nature, resulting in the addition of something or the subtraction of something from the aforesaid [body's] quantity" (*ST* III q. 81 a. 1, *respondio*). And while Aquinas allows that some of the martyrs, like Christ, will have scars of wounds, those who are disabled because they "have been maimed and deprived of their limbs will not be without those limbs in the resurrection of the dead" (*ST* III q. 82 a. 1, ad 1).

Contemporary theologian Amos Yong, who has written extensively on how disability ought to shape our theological imagination, notes the connection between how we construe disability in the eschaton and our present ableist practices:

> If there are no disabilities in the life to come, then that implicitly suggests that our present task is to rid the world of such unfortunate and unwarranted realities. . . . If disability is a reflection of the present, fallen, and broken order

> of things, the redemption of this world and its transformation into the coming eon will involve the removal of all symptoms related to the tragic character of life dominated by sin.

Yong, unlike the care worker in the story about Ian, thinks that "people with intellectual or developmental disabilities, such as those with Down Syndrome or triplicate chromosome 21 – will also retain their phenotypical features in their resurrection bodies" (Yong 2007, 282).

Elsewhere (Timpe 2020) I've argued that at least some disabilities can be present in our resurrected bodies. If there are disabilities that involve, in Elizabeth Barnes' terminology, bad-differences or interfere by their very presence with one's union with God, then for heaven to be the place of ultimate happiness and flourishing, those disabilities would need to be "healed" or "cured." Any state or condition that prevents perfect union with or worship of God will be absent in heaven. But the underlying assumption that all disabilities involve bad-differences is one that I've argued should be rejected.

Consider again Down syndrome (trisomy 21). Down syndrome correlates with heart and gastrointestinal conditions, increased risk for autoimmune disorder, or Alzheimer's. While health is a lot more complex than we often think (see Kukla 2022), perhaps a condition that involves a negative impact on health also involves a bad-difference. But note that these correlations with Down syndrome are just correlations, and not entailed by the condition. There's no reason to think a person with Down syndrome can't have a healthy body. Some might be inclined to think that intellectual disability, a degree of which is found in the vast majority of those with Down syndrome, is what needs to be "healed" in the resurrection. However, the range of human cognitive capacities is broad, even apart from issues related to disability. What range of cognitive abilities are needed for perfect union with God? The higher we set the relevant cognitive bar, the fewer humans will surpass that limit. Better to allow a wide range of intellectual levels to be an acceptable part of human variation. And many individuals with Down syndrome don't appear to be hindered in their union with God, even in this life, by their bodily condition (see Yong 2007). Why think that perfect love isn't compatible with cognitive disability?

Or consider blindness. Certainly blindness can cause, and has caused, a range of harms to individuals; that is, it has decreased their well-being. But the burden is on the person who thinks that decrease in well-being isn't just the result of ableism but instead is primarily about one's union with God to explain why vision is needed for perfect union with God. Are all blind individuals objectively worse off in terms of their union with God in this life because of features intrinsic to the lack of vision? Certainly, individuals with vision impairments encounter harms from nonaccessible physical environments. And much harm also comes from nonaccessible social environments. But surely the Christian hope for the new heaven and the new earth could be made accessible, both physically and socially. Since all the heavenly residents will also be perfected, there's no reason to think this aspect of vision loss will defer one's heavenly joy.

But what, one might ask, about the inherent goods of visual enjoyment? Wouldn't one's heavenly enjoyment be decreased by lack of visual goods, such as being able to enjoy heavenly visual arts that will surpass the glory of even the finest work by Bernini, Rubens, Carivaggio, Grunewald, Fra Angelico, Gaudi, and Terrence Malick? And wouldn't one's heavenly enjoyment also be decreased by not being able to gaze upon the marred, resurrected, and glorified Body of the Incarnate Christ?

As tempting as those questions might be, I think their rhetorical answers are mistaken. First, we need to take seriously the testimony offered by those with vision impairments. In addition to the general testimony by disabled individuals that suggests that disability doesn't impact well-being as much as we might think, there is also literature which suggests that the dominant impact on well-being from vision loss is caused not by the lack of vision itself but rather by lack of social support or receiving only negative support. Second, human sight even without vision impairment is inherently limited. The typical human eye can only recognize electromagnetic radiation with wavelengths from approximately 390 to 700 nm, and there are unsaturated combinations of multiple wavelengths that we also cannot recognize. Will a resurrected human with "normal" vision have their otherwise perfect union with God lessoned because their retinas fail to respond to light with wavelengths of 367 or 731 nm? If the answer is "no," then we need a reason to think that certain wavelengths are essential to human flourishing in heaven, while others are not. Third, imagine an individual with vision impairment who is aware that they are missing out on some human goods despite being in heaven. Would that awareness be sufficient to detract from the beatific vision? It's not clear that it would be. If the fullness of the beatific vision is compatible with awareness of the atrocities of human history and, at least on traditional Christian views about hell, the eternal lack of the beatific vision that those in hell suffer, the beatific vision would likely also be compatible with the absence of certain created visual goods. To think that perfect union with God will be lessened by the lack of visual access to certain wavelengths of electromagnetic radiation may be to misunderstand the nature of our heavenly goodness.

There are reasons then to reject the view that all disabled bodies need to be "healed" or "cured" in the resurrection for union with God on the Christian worldview. While the evidence I've given for the possibility of disabled resurrection bodies is admittedly speculative, such a limitation is inherent to theological reflection on eschatological bodies. Furthermore, what I've suggested aligns with the testimony of many disabled individuals about their own experience of their bodies in the present life. Taking seriously the possibility of resurrected disabled bodies can help us avoid some of the negative assumptions that have pervaded much of Church history (e.g., the conflation of disability and sin, tropes of virtuous suffering, segregationist, and exclusionary models of "charity"), even if the acceptance of heavenly disability isn't strictly necessary for avoiding these negatives. Given that our eschatology shapes our present Christian practices, viewing disability as something that always requires "curing" makes it easier to devalue the lives of those with disabilities.

3 The Wider Context of Embodiment

3.1 The Range of Human Embodiment

Section 1 argued that at times we tend to ignore our bodies, while at others we consider them but only in idealized ways. Section 2 sought to resist both of those tendencies by examining disability in the context of embodiment. As these previous discussions should make clear, there is not a single unified way either of being embodied or of responding to embodiment. Talk about "the body" can misleadingly suggest that there is one experience of what it's like to be embodied. And the default body that is assumed, even if only implicitly, is often as Cressida Heyes puts it: "something stripped of its historical and social context – not only a male body, but also a white European body; an aesthetically normative body; a nondisabled body; a human body; or even an extra-cognitive, corpse-like body whose very existence contributes nothing of value to philosophical projects" (Heyes 2021, 350).

How we conceive of embodiment is a socially and politically shaped concept, influenced by other views and value judgments that people have. Psychologist Seymour Fisher, perhaps best known for his work on the female orgasm, noted decades ago that a visibly disabled body is often "viewed as simultaneously inferior and threatening. He [sic.] becomes associated with the special class of monster images that haunts each culture" (Fisher 1973, 73). Cultural meanings and associations such as those noted by Fisher can operate below the surface, without criticism or even outright explicit awareness. To put this point in terms of David Foster Wallace's metaphor introduced in Section 2, the kind of embodiment that occupies dominant social positions can easily become our "water," where we assume that this is what all bodies should be like. As author, activist, and slam poet Sonya Renee Taylor writes, "the default body becomes the template for the normal body" (Taylor 2018, 32). This expectation of what bodies should be like often operates only in the background, suggesting that it is part of the conceptual frame that carries normative force. Bodies that live up to this expected norm are assumed to have greater value, including sometimes moral value, and prestige.

But the truth is there is a wide range that human embodiment can take. Even biological sex isn't the clear binary that many folks take it to be (Dea 2016), and feminist philosophers have discussed how the embodiments of gender are historical contingencies. Similarly, bodies have been racialized in ways that often serve the exploitation of one group by another dominating group (Grimes 2016). Bodies that are sufficiently unlike ours are often interpreted by us as abject, resulting in revulsion, fear, or disgust (see Kristiva 1982 for an influential discussion of abjection). Our lived embodiment then depends not only on what our bodies are actually like but also on what those around us expect our bodies to be like and how they respond to them. Our bodies can "misfit" or fail to conform to the expectations of our environment (Wieseler 2019; Holmes 2020). Since bodies have political meaning, having one's body taken to be nonconfirming can come with consequences. Feminist philosopher Clare Chambers observes that the body is "the surface on which we're expected to inscribe our identities. Its appearance gives or denies access to various positions of privilege, membership of social groups, indicators of esteem" (Chambers 2022, 5). Forms of embodiment that do not live up to larger social expectations can lead to ostracism, mistreatment, or even abuse.

Jacqueline Urla and Jennifer Terry suggest the terminology of "deviant bodies" for those who do not live up to the cultural assumption of what bodies should be like. As they use the term, it is both a characteristic of bodies and the "historically and culturally specific belief that deviant social behavior, however exactly that is defined, manifests in the materiality of the body, as a cause or an effect, our perhaps as merely a suggestive trace" (Urla and Terry 1995, 2); similarly disability scholar Tobin Siebers writes of "markers of corporeal deviation" that tend to result in social isolation (Siebers 2003, 952). We often interpret bodies that deviate from this culturally assumed norm as reflecting problematic behavior or moral status, a tendency which political scientist Harlan Hahn has traced at least as far back as the nineteenth century (Hahn 1995). Quill Kukla locates the attempt to read moral character from the aesthetics of one's body as far back as the seventeenth century. How exactly this plays out is closely connected with cultural tendencies toward racism and sexism: "the raced and gendered body is deeply infected with moral and social meanings" (Kukla 2009, 78). Using Urla and Terry's language of "deviant body" isn't intended to suggest that one has actually done something morally wrong if one's body fails to live up to dominant social expectations. But there are social pressure that act *as if* that evaluative judgment is accurate. These pressures and expectations can be internalized so that individuals are not only treated as if their bodies are problematic but can also feel that judgment themselves. There are many ways for bodies to be judged deviate and to reinforce the judgment that nondeviant bodies are more valuable. (For historical discussions, see Thomson 1996 and Thomson 1997.)

For instance, consider the wide range of pop culture villains represented as fat: *Star Wars*' Jabba the Hutt, the entire Dursley family from *Harry Potter*, Marvel's Kingpin, and DC's Penguin. In addition to Ursula from *The Little Mermaid*, Disney has a long history of fat characters portrayed as buffoonish, pitiable, or malicious: Queen of Hearts from *Alice in Wonderland*, Smee from *Peter Pan*, and LeFou from *Beauty and the Beast*. Or consider how scarring and other forms of physical disfigurement are also used to signal villainy: Scar from *The Lion King*; Safin, Alec Trevelyan, Raoul Silva, and Zao are all facially disfigured James Bond villains; or the mutilation of Anikin Skywalker's body as he becomes Darth Vader in *Star Wars* and goes over to "the Dark Side." Scholars have noted that a wide range of disabilities are negatively portrayed in media (Holcomb and Latham-Mintus 2022; Swartz et al. 2013; Grue 2023).

Amanda Leduc's book *Disfigured: On Fairy Tales, Disability, and Making Space* examines fairy tales, both classic and as presented by Disney, and contemporary films in terms of how they portray not only disability but also beauty and age. Deformed, ugly, or old bodies often are used to indicate bad moral character (Leduc 2020). Many of these characters, from the hag in *Snow White* to Marvel's Red Skull, illustrate "the idea that the body is an external expression of an inner self" (Murray 2008, 26f). Even in fairy tales where the character with the deviant body ends up being the protagonist, their eventual success is because of some feat they have done and not because society learns to accept them as they are:

> Instead of imbuing the reader with a worldview in which change is possible and things can turn out positively for the disenfranchised, the prevalence of magic in fairy tales serves to reinforce the class and societal structures already in place, as well as traditional ideas of what it means to have a functioning body in the world. This is possibly why there's almost always a price that a protagonist pays for the magic of their transformation. You cannot simply move from one place to the next – society won't allow it. And so the protagonist must prove their worthiness – through good deeds and gentle behavior, as in the case of Cinderella, or, as with the Little Mermaid, through sacrifice and trial. (Leduc 2020, 42)

Deviant bodies may be accepted, but only if their worth can first be proven.

3.2 Deviant Embodiments

It would be good, in contrast, if we had a societal understanding that valued a wide range of bodies. This is especially true when one looks not only at fairy tales and movies but also at the actual embodied lives of people. Harlan Hahn notes that it is "increasingly evident" (Hahn 1995, 395) that bodies judged to be deviant need to be the focus of scholarship and advocacy work in order to change their stigmatization. We'll thus explore a number of kinds of embodiment that historically have been taken to be deviant.

3.2.1 Ugly Bodies

I begin with bodies that are judged to be "ugly." Historically, many physically disabled bodies have been seen as ugly precisely because they are disabled. According to Jasmine Harris, the "aesthetics of disability" shape not only how others approach and understand disabled bodies but also how those bodies are integrated into society and often what legal rights they are given. Civil War veterans who had an arm or leg amputated as the result of the war tended not to hide their disabilities, instead favoring tightly pinned-up empty pant legs or sleeves. But as the war receded from the immediate past, public response to visible disabilities rapidly changed. Consider, for instance, what have come to be called "the Ugly Laws," a series of laws passed by cities in the latter parts of the nineteenth century and into the twentieth century that criminalized the presence of visible forms of disability in public spaces. Though not the first, Chicago's ugly law passed in 1881 is perhaps the best known:

> Any person who is diseased, maimed, mutilated, or in any way deformed, so as to be an unsightly or disgusting object, or an improper person to be allowed in or on the streets, highways, thoroughfares, or public places this city, shall not therein or thereon expose himself to public view under the penalty of a fine. (Schweik 2009, 1f)

Notice that the wording of the law refers to those who are "diseased, maimed, mutilated, or in any way deformed" as "improper persons" and even "disgusting objects." San Francisco's ugly law made it illegal for "any person, who is diseased, maimed, mutilated or deterred in any way, so as to be an unsightly or disgusting object" to be in a public space, further reducing such people to mere objects. Susan M. Schweik discusses how such laws treated people's bodily aesthetics as a "badge of moral depravity" (Schweik 2009, 27). Five years after San Francisco's ugly law was passed, concerned about the influx of disabled Chinese immigrants, the state of California enacted a law limiting immigration for those deemed to be a "lunatic, idiot, deaf, blind, cripple or infirm person" (Schweik 2009, 167). New Orlean's ugly law referred to an individual with a visible disability in public as "an idle and disorderly person, and . . . a rogue and a vagabond" (Schweik 2009, 32f). (It should be noted that according to Schweik, the last documented arrest in the United States via one of these laws was in Omaha, Nebraska in 1974, a year after an amendment to the federal Vocational Rehabilitation Act outlawed discrimination on the basis of disability; see Schweik 2009, 6.)

Legal scholar Jasmine E. Harris notes that "the aesthetics of disability trigger affective processes, however, and some emotions, such as fear or disgust, make it hard to recognize, respect, adjudicate, and enforce the rights of people with disabilities" (Harris 2019, 897). Aesthetic judgments about bodies shape interpersonal interactions. "These physical and sensory markers of difference – for instance, facial disfigurement, non-normative speech, or . . . atypical behavior – produce emotional responses (for example, fear, attraction, contempt, disgust) that are often viewed as noncognitive, visceral, and thus involuntary reactions" (Harris 2019, 904). Aesthetic judgments about bodies are not *merely* individual judgments or preferences. They get encoded into interpersonal dynamics, social norms, and sometimes even mediate legal rights.

The aesthetics of disabled bodies are also deeply connected with beliefs and judgments about sex, gender, race, and class. As the advocates who worked to repeal the Ugly Laws and make space for public display of disability achieved a measure of success, social policies and cultural beliefs about disability would also change, though slowly. According to historian Brad Byron, "by claiming public space on the sidewalks of urban centers, destitute cripples had made an effective political statement" (Byrom 2004, 29).

The idealization of the aesthetics of the body, even apart from disability, often serves as the locus for economic exchange or profit. One study by the National Bureau of Economic Research found that individuals deemed "strikingly beautiful or handsome," holding constant other demographics and labor-market characteristics, are paid as much as 13 percent more than those whose looks are considered "average"; and the penalty for being deemed unattractive was found to be even greater (Hamermesh and Biddle 1993). The researchers found that "better-looking people sort into occupations where beauty is more likely to be more productive; but the impact of individuals' looks on their earnings is mostly independent of occupation" (Hamermesh and Biddle 1993, abstract). Other studies have a similar "beauty pay gap," which perhaps surprisingly tends to be greater for men than for women (Sierminska 2015; Pfeifer 2012). And a range of feminist texts have connected expectations regarding female beauty with patriarchal systems; see, among others, I. M. Young (1990), Wolf (1991), Widdows (2018), and Chambers (2022).

3.2.2 Fat Bodies

Abigail Saguy's *What's Wrong with Fat?* documents various conceptual frames within which fatness and obesity are understood in contemporary Western culture. Much of the public views fatness through an "immorality frame" where it is condemned as a marker of personal moral failing, often specifically the vices of sloth or gluttony. Fatness is not only *bad*, it's seen to be the person's own fault for which they deserve moral blame. Being deemed as "fat," that is, is taken to indicate a moral failing for which the individual alone is responsible. (Never mind, of course, that the virtue tradition in ethics has long held that virtues are developed in communities and often require the wisdom and training of others, thus making the fostering of virtue an inherently communal project.) And this despite research showing that genetics account for at least 70 percent of the variance in body mass across the human population.

Saguy's research has found that while much of Europe shares the United States' emphasis on obesity as a medical epidemic, the emphasis on individual moral blame is higher in the United States than in other countries. Cases of "fit fatness" are ignored. People who are thin but engage in the behavior patterns for which fat persons are usually castigated – sedentary lifestyle, junk food, and so on – are also ignored. In this context, "fatness has long been associated with lack of control, immorality, barbarity, and blackness. . . . In the United States, the stigmatization of fatness and adulation of thinness were interrelated and profoundly raced, classed, and gendered processes" (Saguy 2013, 40f). Others, such as Mollow (2022) and Jacobs (2023), connect fatphobia and ableism. And while psychology research associated with Harvard University's implicit bias tests have found a decline in racist, sexist, and ableist scores over the course of a decade, anti-fat bias has increased in both implicit and explicit attitudes, the former as much as 40 percent (Gordon 2020, 3 and 24). While BMI as the leading measure of obesity has been widely shown to not track health, "nearly all academic and scientific research that has looked for a link between weight stigma (including concern trolling) and ill health has found it" (Gordon 2020, 78; see also Tylka et al. 2014).

Saguy notes that her own thinness has worked to her favor, "mak[ing] me more credible in my critical analysis of the dominant framing of obesity" (Saguy 2013, 35). Another fat studies scholar, Samantha Murray, says that numerous medical professionals have misdiagnosed some of her health issues as resulting from her perceived "fatness" (Murray 2008, 37 and 76). Other similar stories abound, with fat patients, especially women, having their symptoms downplayed or ignored by doctors who fail to accurately diagnose the real cause of their illness and instead put all the blame for the individual's ailments on their weight. Laura Young and Brian Powell's sociological research found that "doctors expressed a preference not to advise and/or treat the extremely overweight patient in part because the physicians viewed obesity as an indicated of several undesirable qualities, including lack of control. . . . Obese clients are evaluated more negatively than are their normal weight counterparts" (L. M. Young and Powell 1985, 234 and 241). These findings are consistent with what others have found (see Phelan et al. 2015 for recent review articles and Manne 2024, chapter 2 for an extended discussion). Many people, women especially, delay doctors' appointments out of the desire to lose weight first.

And lest one think this behavior is irrational, it is often for good reason. One study of over 4,700 medical students found explicit anti-fat bias in nearly 67 percent of study participants, and implicit anti-fat bias in 74 percent (Phelan et al. 2014). Anti-fat bias has led some doctors' offices to set bodyweight limits for patients. Fat people also face discrimination in employment, transportation, and therapy (Gordon 2020). One study regarding salary, for instance, found that fat women "earned $9,000 less than their average-weight counterparts, [and] very heavy women earned $19,000 less" (McGee 2014). Very thin women, by contrast, earned $22,000 more than average. And as recently as 2020, it was legal in 48 of the United States to fire, refuse to hire, or to deny housing to someone on the basis of their being fat (Gordon 2020, 27; Martin 2017).

Both Saguy and Murray note how society's responses to fat bodies are gendered. One only needs to turn toward diet and food advertising to see this gendering at work. The cultural expectation of thinness for women differs from the more muscled physique that is valorized as the mark of masculinity. Women who don't live up to or approach this normative expectation are often deemed to be moral failures. Murray, for instance, writes:

> The "fat" woman (is presumed to be) lazy, she is out of control, she is a moral failure, she is unhealthy, she is an affront to normative feminine bodily aesthetics, she is a food addict, she cannot manage her desires, her level of intelligence is below average. . . . These assumptions are embodied at the level of perception, and therefore inform our reading of bodies. (Murray 2008, 13f)

Kate Manne's recent *UnShrinking* is an extended discussion of fatphobia and how it is embedded in a wide range of cultural assumptions about value, intersecting with misogyny, racism, classism, and ableism. "Fatphobia," she writes, "is an inherently structural phenomenon, which sees people in fatter bodies navigating a different world, containing numerous distinct material, social, and institutional barriers to our flourishing" (Manne 2024, 12). For instance, Manne points to studies that show bias by teachers against fat students, "deem[ing] them less academically capable, despite unchanging objective measures in the form of their standardized test scores" (Manne 2024, 19, referencing Sole-Smith 2023 and Kenney et al. 2015).

As with other kinds of stigma and oppression aimed at deviant bodies, fatphobia's effects are systemic and lifelong. As a result, three dozen international medical researchers recently publishes a consensus statement in the journal *Nature Medicine*, endorsed by over fifty international scientific societies and organizations. It pointed out that fat stigma not only negatively impacts individuals but can also "exert negative influences on public health policies, access to treatments, and research" (Rubino et al. 2020, 486; for a recent discussion of how to better accommodate fat persons' needs in a wide array of health care settings, see Hardy 2023).

3.2.3 Sick and Scarred Bodies

Another kind of embodiment that is stigmatized relates to health. Given the cultural tendency to wrongly think that to be disabled is to be sick, ill, or otherwise unhealthy, disabled people often have to disclose personal information, including health information, in order to secure various accommodations. Disabled painter and author Riva Lehrer describes this process in her memoir, *Golem Girl*:

> I often feel that Disabled people are expected – compelled – to disclose every medical detail, the more embarrassing, the better. It gives us credibility and feeds the voyeurism embedded in medical narratives. I understand that we all deal with mortality through others' stories of illness and injury (just as horror films and disaster flicks help us manage our fears), but this sort of expectation creates a compulsory humiliation. (Lehrer 2020, 276 note 1)

While some disabilities can cause chronic health problems and some illnesses can disable, both disability advocates like Lehrer and scholars such as Susan Wendell have pushed back against the identification of disability and illness or poor health in general. It is possible, Wendell argues, to be "healthy disabled" (Wendell 2001). Even apart from issues related to disability, bioethics reveals that health is actually much more complex than many initially think; and many things that are often taken to be constitutive of or markers of health, like BMI, turn out not to be. Health, Eli Clare writes, "is a mire" (Clare 2017, 14; see also Kukla 2022).

As Havi Carel notes in her *Illness: The Cry of the Flesh*, illness can change how we experience our own bodies when they're sick, as well as how others regard them. Both of these aspects can lead to estrangement. Regarding the first aspect, she writes: "Illness changes not only the experience, by limiting it, or making it painful, but also its structure. The experience of space and time, for example, is modified in many somatic and mental disorders. . . . Illness also calls into question the meaning-making we routinely engage in" (Carel 2019, xii).

Carel also notes that illness reveals that it's not our diseased bodies but rather our experience of them that matters more. Two people can have this same illness and yet have very different experiences, which reveals how significant the interpretation of bodies, including our own, is. For this reason, she favors a phenomenological rather than naturalistic approach to sick bodies. When we take note of the experience of sick bodies, we recognize, similar to disabled bodies, that our social structures and lives are not set up for sick bodies, but instead presuppose healthy – that is, "normal" – bodies.

Not all sick or ill bodies are considered deviant in the way I'm using the phrase here. As I write, my spouse has a relatively minor illness that has not resulted in any stigmatization. While many adults prefer not to deal with other adults' mucus or emesis, that is primarily a preference that doesn't rise to the level of mistreatment. (In contrast, many folks do in fact stigmatize other adults for their incontinence, catheterization, or colostomy bags.) However, a number of excellent books recount what it's like to live with and through breast cancer. These texts reveal that cancerous bodies, especially women's bodies with cancer in highly sexualized breast tissue, are often stigmatized and treated as deviant.

Audre Lorde's *The Cancer Journals* brings into focus how differently we treat different types of amputations depending on larger cultural norms and values regarding bodies. Lorde was a queer black American poet, writer, and professor who was diagnosed with breast cancer at the age of forty-four. Lorde's treatment required an amputation of her right breast, a modified radical mastectomy. Lorde was then pressured by friends and medical staff alike to undergo reconstructive surgery or somehow otherwise hide the results of her mastectomy. People presumed she would opt for either a "mask of prosthesis or the dangerous fantasy of reconstruction," but in her view either would be "a cosmetic sham" (Lorde 1980, 9). In the hospital, she was urged by staff and a woman from Reach for Recovery, a peer support program from the American Cancer Society, to use "a wad of lambswool pressed into a page pink breast-shaped pad. . . . Her message was, you are just as good as you were before because you can look exactly the same" (Lorde 1980, 34). This suggestion struck Lorde as inane, as "a pathetic puff of lambswool . . . has no relationship nor likeness to her own breasts" (Lorde 1980, 52). On another day, Lorde was told by a nurse at her doctor's office, "You will feel much better with it on. . . . And besides, we really like you to wear something, at least when you come in. Otherwise it's bad for the moral of the office" (Lorde 1980, 52). But Lorde questioned why other people's preferences for her embodiment should be what shaped her behavior. Lorde would reject the use of a prosthesis or form because of the implications it would have for understanding our embodiment. As she put it in her journal: "This emphasis upon the cosmetic after surgery reinforces this society's stereotype of women, that we are only what we look or appear, so this is the only aspect of our existence we need to address" (Lorde 1980, 50).

Relatedly, Anne Boyer notes in her Pulitzer Prize winning *The Undying* that the cultural response to sick bodies, and how they present in public, is rooted not only in medicine but also in ideology (Boyer 2019). While Lorde didn't think there was anything wrong with a prosthetic, her concern was with the social pressures and assumptions that come from that underlying ideology. Part of the specific pressure on women to "appear whole" after a mastectomy comes from the cultural pressure to view women's bodies as objects of sexual desire. Lorde described it this way: "attitudes toward the necessity for prostheses after breast surgery are merely a reflection of those attitudes within our society towards women in general as objectified and depersonalized sexual conveniences" (Lorde 1980, 57). Unlike other prosthetics that aim at functionality, false breasts, like glass eyes, are only about appearance. Lorde refused to think of breast cancer as primarily a cosmetic problem. For her, it was instead an issue of human finitude and the limited time we have for our projects and with those we love. For her, cancer was a reminder of the need to live a considered life open to our own mortality.

Lorde compares the way our culture treats a woman's amputation of a breast to other amputations:

> When Moishe Dayan, the Prime Minster of Israel, stands up in front of parliament or on TV with an eyepatch over his empty eye socket, nobody tells him to go get a glass eye, or that he is bad for the moral of the office. If you have trouble dealing with Moishe Dayan's empty eye socket, everyone recognizes that it is your problem to solve, not his. (Lorde 1980, 52f)

Society interprets Dayan's lost eye, as with many amputations resulting from war, as an honorable wound, as evidence of bravery or valor. My father-in-law had a prosthetic leg due to an amputation from the Korean War. His most recent leg was designed for increased functionality rather than to look as much like a regular leg as possible. When he'd wear it with shorts, and especially with a hat indicating that he was a veteran, he'd regularly have people coming up to him expressing their gratitude for his service. This shows that the response to scarred and disfigured bodies depends on the larger set of values, commitments, and conceptual frames our society has.

3.3 An Even Wider Range

The particular kinds of devalued embodiments examined here are not exhaustive. There are also other kinds of embodiment that lead to mistreatment: racialized bodies, trans bodies, neurodivergent and and mentally ill bodies that are stigmatized based on their behaviors or appearance. There are yet even more kinds of embodied experiences – pregnancy, infancy, old age – that are also devalued even if not resulting in oppression. Given how wide the range embodiment can take is, it may "no longer [be] viable to talk about 'the human body' as a single, universal entity. Indeed, as it turns out, to do so is to comply with an agenda of domination through reduction" (Urla and Terry 1995, 4). Those aspects of embodiment that remind us of our dependence and finitude especially tend to provoke such a response. It is to this topic that we now turn.

4 Embodied Dependence

4.1 Varieties of Dependence

So far, this Element has argued for the importance of taking seriously the range of human embodiment, rather than focusing too much on idealized understandings that can lead to stigmatization and mistreatment. Conceptual frames were introduced in Section 2, which also discussed how some of our frames regarding disabled bodies are problematic. This was expanded in Section 3 to consider a wide range that embodiment can take. We often don't notice some of the conceptual frames that shape how we think about embodiment, which can then shape not only our evaluations of others but also a range of our practices.

Because we are embodied, we are inherently dependent beings. Our dependence makes us vulnerable, and so relations of care are also central to the human experience. But all bodies are not equally dependent or equally vulnerable. Sometimes our vulnerability is a function of facts about our bodies. At other times, however, our vulnerability is a function of how others treat us in virtue of our bodies. Because we value different kinds of embodiment differently, we also don't think about the resulting kinds of dependence in the same way. We need to take seriously, as bioethicist O. Carter Snead writes, "the vulnerability, mutual dependence, and finitude that results from our individual and shared lives as embodied beings" (Snead 2020, 7). Unfortunately, much of the theorizing in philosophy of religion and philosophical theology has tended to ignore or undervalue the importance of human dependence and the care that it calls for. Sandra Sullivan-Dunbar has argued that significant portions of contemporary Christian ethics have failed to take seriously enough human dependence, both in terms of the demands of love and of justice. This "marginalization of dependency within Christian ethics," she argues, "is an injustice to those who engage in the moral work of dependent care on a daily basis" (Sullivan-Dunbar 2017, 2). This section canvasses what we can learn about human dependence by taking seriously the range of human embodiment.

Part of what it means to be human as embodied beings is to be finite. Elija Milligram contrasts idealized approaches to human embodiment and agency, introduced in Section 1, with what he refers to as "bounded agency": "Not only is all real-world agency . . . *bounded*, and not only should we try to make sense of the varied forms of bounded agency on their own terms, without seeing them as deviations from an ideal; we should not be trying to articulate a conception of ideal agency" (Millgram 2022, 68). In thinking about what humans are like, we need to take seriously a range of ways in which we are dependent, bounded by the kinds of embodiments we possess.

Snead notes that it's important to think about human embodiment "in light of what and who we really are" (Snead 2020, 2). I agree. Humans are fundamentally dependent beings, and in a number of different ways. Our dependence includes, at the least:

1. Dependence on the structure of the physical world,
2. Dependence on others, and
3. Dependence on God.

As we shall see, these various dependencies are related to each other. I shall argue, in Section 5, that they shape the moral demands that arise from embodiment.

4.1.1 Physical Dependence

Humans are embodied agents. Since our bodies are physical, we too are physical agents. By this I do not mean to say that we are *purely* physical beings. As discussed in Section 1, dualist views think that humans are most fundamentally immaterial souls that can interact with physical bodies. In addition, there is a range of views about human nature according to which we are partly but not entirely physical. Aristotle and Aquinas, for instance, have a view of human persons, and of physical substances more generally, on which they are compounds of form (*eidos* or *morphê* in Greek) and matter (*hulê* in Greek). On this view, living things like humans have as their substantial form a soul (*psyche* in Greek), understood not as a separate substance but as the principle of life. Other philosophers object even to this kind of dualism, often called hylomorphic (from *hulê* and *morphê*) dualism. Instead they think that humans are purely physical or material beings. In calling human embodiment physical, I mean for the term to stretch to include both of these general approaches.

Humans, as physical beings in this specified sense, are bounded, to use Millgram's language, by the nature of the physical world. While philosophy might be able to show us that we are dependent in this way, it along can't tell us everything about what that means. To have a complete understanding of human embodiment and the physical dependence it entails, we must look beyond philosophy and also take seriously the insights of other disciplines. This includes what we know about the nature of the physical world through physics and chemistry and biology. To properly understand the nature of human embodiment, we have to understand the physical world in which our bodies exist, develop, and hopefully thrive. We are subject to gravity, entropy, and all sorts of causal interactions. Human flesh will dissolve in lye or hydrofluoric acid. Too much pressure will crush us. Another way our agency is bounded is by the kinds of bodies we have. Humans cannot fly unaided, for instance, because our bodies lack wings. We cannot breathe underwater in virtue of having lungs rather than gills. To continue to be living embodied agents, we need an environment that contains sufficient oxygen, sufficient nutrition, the right range of temperatures, and so on. Our physical dependence means that we are vulnerable in a number of ways: "By virtue of our [specific form of embodiment], human beings have bodily and material needs; are exposed to physical illness, injury, disability, and death" (Mackenzie et al. 2014b, 1). To put the point another way, we are dependent on a wide range of physical, chemical, and biological conditions for our existence and our continued survival.

We are not able to change this fundamental fact of our physical dependence on the world. This then gives us reason to care about the future of the physical world. Yet we have reason to worry about various parts of our environment: climate change, deforestation, declines in biodiversity, and the bee crisis. We also have reason to make sure that people have access to what they need to meet their physical needs, from proper nutrition to health care. This then points us in the direction of the second sense of dependence.

4.1.2 Social Dependence

Physical factors are not the only constraints we face. We are also bounded as social beings. While it is possible that we grow all of our own food, few if any of us do. We depend on others to grow the coffee beans we need for our morning double espresso and the wheat that becomes our morning toast. We depend on our biological parents for our conception. Many, though not all of us, depend on the same parents for the care we received as infants, and for our early moral formation. We depend on others for our education. We depend on complex economic systems to produce and distribute the wide range of physical goods that we need, value, and consume. We depend on increasingly complicated medical systems and public services to provide various goods when we're sick, injured, old, or disabled. Furthermore, those systems don't make access to the goods that they provide easily. For some of them, there are active gatekeeping mechanisms aimed at making access to the socially provided goods difficult to secure. In such cases, there is often the need to depend on others, such as case managers and social workers, to help those who depend on care systems to gain access. Jackie Leach Scully puts the point this way:

> Few of us could survive, let alone thrive, even as healthy, able-bodied adults, if we had to do absolutely everything for ourselves that we needed to. (And even if we would, most of us would find it an intensely demanding, precarious, and probably tedious form of life.) In anything but very rudimentary or transient groupings, people are supported in a dense network of dependencies for food, light, heat, housing, communication, friendship, love, education, policing, transport, rubbish disposal, health care, and one and one. We live in groups because that's how we live best. (Scully 2014, 213)

To be human is to be a social being and dependent on other humans for our wellbeing. And this makes us susceptible to various kinds of structural inequalities such as racism, ableism, or misogyny.

In one sense, humans aren't unique in being socially dependent. Meerkat pups depend on other meerkats. Bees depend on other bees. While many species from ants to orcas exhibit social behavior, human social behavior tends to be more complex. Research has shown that aspects of our social behavior, such as aggression and hierarchy, depend on the quantities of various neurotransmitters like serotonin and oxytocin (S. N. Young 2008). One upshot of this research is that the physical and the social are not always easily disentangled.

One fundamental aspect of human social dependence is cooperation. We are, as a recent issue of *Nature Human Behavior* put it, reliant "on cooperation to survive and thrive" ("The Cooperative Human" 2018, 427). The ways that humans depend on each other changes throughout the course of our lives. At various times of our lives we are more or less dependent on others for the receiving of care. One of the consequences of our dependence on others, and their dependence on us, is obligations of care. What specific obligations of care we have with others depends on the specifics of our relationship with each one of them. Some of these obligations are negative in that we have the obligation *not* to treat people in certain ways. We should not treat others as mere means to our own ends or objects for our own consumption. Other obligations are positive. We are obligated to act in service of others' physical need even at the expense of our own personal comfort. (Unfortunately, this is an obligation that I too often fail to satisfy.) We are obligated to contribute to various public goods that we benefit from, even if the exact form of that contribution can vary.

Our interactions with and dependence on others depend on bodies. To quote bioethicist Carter Snead again, "our embodiment situates us in a particular relationship to one another" (Snead 2020, 3). It's important to note, however, that as with various kinds of embodiment, we treat some kinds of social dependency differently. The evaluation of the acceptability of social dependence depends on, among other factors, age. Infants and, to a lesser degree, the elderly are understood to have higher social dependency needs than do others. But the specific amount of social dependence a person has is a function of much more than just age. Individuals with various kinds of disabilities, for instance, might have increased dependence on others for a range of needed care. For some, this is social dependence on others for transportation. In other cases, it involves dependence on others for dressing or bathing or toileting. And here, various forms of stigma and hierarchy come up again. Racially advantaged white males tend to be thought to be more independent than minority women. This is, in part, a result of how we think of dependence that requires care work as the paradigm of dependence, even if dependence is much broader. "Dependence as care has been pathologized, rather than recognized as part of our human condition" (Chatzidakis et al. 2020, 23). As a result, there is immense pressure to avoid certain kinds of dependency that are tied to the stigma attached to certain bodies rather than a recognition of dependence as an intrinsic part of the human condition.

Consider, for instance, the pressure to avoid having a child with Down syndrome, which usually involves increased social dependence for the rest of that individual's life. The most common prenatal screening for Down syndrome at present is amniocentesis, which is a standard part of prenatal care in many countries. Studies suggest that 67 percent of positive prenatal diagnoses in the United States end in selective abortion, while the rate is over 90 percent in some European countries (Natoli et al. 2012). Amniocentesis itself carries with it a risk of spontaneous abortion. Furthermore, data suggests that fetuses who have Down syndrome detected by prenatal screening are more likely to abort spontaneously than are fetuses with Down syndrome that are not detected prenatally

(Leporrier et al. 2003). More recent technology, such as noninvasive prenatal testing can now do such diagnostic work using only maternal blood rather than extracting amniotic fluid as required by amniocentesis, thereby eliminating the primary risk of prenatal testing. The pressures to avoid having a child with Down syndrome will likely increase given the reduction in risk.

Commenting on these pressures, bioethicist Chris Kaposy notes: "People with physical and cognitive needs that make them dependent [beyond what we expect for all humans] have long been marginalized in Western culture and political discourse. . . . By valuing the capacities of independence, the standing of dependent people – such as those with cognitive disabilities – becomes marginal" (Kaposy 2018, 145).

Those who need increased levels of care become the object of pity or charity. Charity then becomes stigmatized, especially in certain dimensions of political discourse. Kaposy continues: "social programs such as welfare are [often] seen as handouts, as getting 'something for nothing', an unjustifiable reward for laziness. People receiving social assistance are seen as 'takers' rather than 'makers'" (Kaposy 2018, 45). Notice however that the ability to contribute to economic exchange is itself a function of social dependence.

Stigmatized forms of social dependence results in care work that often come at the expense of other individuals rather than from political structures. This in turn reinforces the social pressure to not have children who will be dependent in this way, reinforcing the cultural pressure to avoid having children with Down syndrome, a pressure which some of Kaposy's work confirms (Kaposy 2019). But the problem with this way of accepting only some kinds of dependence as appropriate is

> that it fails to acknowledge the degree to which we are all dependent on one another, disabled and nondisabled alike. The distinction between those who are independent and those who are dependent is untenable. . . . We are all dependent at different moments in our lives. This fact is hard for many of us to accept because of the value we place on our ability to control our lives and futures. . . . But this power of control is fragile and fleeting, if it exists at all. (Kaposy 2018, 146)

Even though we're all socially dependent, we're not all socially dependent in the same way and to the same degree. As with various forms of embodiment, some forms of dependence are seen to be problematic, while others are taken to be normal or even not recognized as forms of dependence at all. "Commonly shared dependencies," Jackie Leach Scully notes, "become genuinely invisible" (Scully 2014, 216). Less common forms too often result in marginalization.

Some scholars try to differentiate dependence from *inter*dependence, the latter of which is undertaken voluntarily, such as in economic exchange. Eva Kittay refers to this as "the pretense that we are *independent* – that the cooperation between persons that some insist is *inter*dependence is simply the mutual (often voluntary) cooperation between essentially independent persons" (Kittay 1998, xii). Instead, to be human is, in fact, to be dependent on other humans. Rich people depend on all kinds of workers (e.g., domestic workers) and financial systems for their own free time and maintenance of their wealth, though these forms of social dependence are often not recognized as such.

4.1.3 Dependence on God

All three of the world's major monotheisms, as well as a number of other religious traditions, affirm that embodied humans, as part of creation, also are fundamentally dependent upon God. At the heart of the Christian faith, for instance, is the claim "that we have been created for a second-personal relationship to God. Not only is the fulfillment of this need integral to our flourishing; it is not possible to provide an account of what it is to be human that does not recognize this" (Torrance 2022, ix). The Christian scriptures place human dependence and vulnerability at the heart of salvation history (see, for instance, Cooreman-Guittin 2021 for a reading of key aspects of the biblical texts that take into account human dependence and vulnerability). For Christians, human redemption, sanctification, and eternal flourishing all depend upon God's salvific acts.

But human dependence and vulnerability aren't merely the result of sin; they are instead part of what it means to be created as human. It is not possible, as a human, to cease to be dependent given our nature as creation. All of creation, including embodied humans, depends upon God for its coming into existence. Christianity has traditionally held that God creates ex nihilo, that is out of nothing. In this way, calling humans "dependent creatures" is redundant (see Kapic 2022, 10). Furthermore, God's evaluation of creation, including its dependency, is that it is *good* (Genesis 1:31).

The doctrine of divine conservation, sometimes also referred to as continuous creation, holds that creation is not only dependent upon God's creative act for coming into existence in the first place but that creation is also dependent upon God for its being kept in existence. Apart from God's conserving things in existence, no created entity would continue to exist. As Jonathan Kvanvig and Hugh McCann describe the doctrine of divine conservation, "God continually sustains the universe at every instant of its existence. Further, His sustenance of it is not merely an effect of some other or previous action; it is the direct result of

His present involvement in the world" (Kvanvig and McCann 1988, 13). While some might think that once God creates something, that thing has its own independent existence, such a view is, they continue, "from the point of view of philosophical theology, unorthodox. The orthodox position would seem to be that the things God creates have no more capacity to continue in existence than to bring themselves to be" (Kvanvig and McCann 1988, 14). They argue that no created substance can be self-sustaining (though for an attempted defense of existential inertia, see Beaudoin 2007).

A stronger claim than divine conservation is that of occasionalism, which holds that God is the only causal force that acts on creation. Occasionalism entails divine conservation, though one can endorse divine conservation without being an occasionalist. Jonathan Edwards was an influential Christian occasionalist (see Crisp and Strobel 2018 for a discussion of Edwards' view). Many Islamic theologians and philosophers have also endorsed occasionalism, though some of the latter, holding that creation is eternal, have done so without also endorsing divine creation out of nothing (see Salim and Malik 2022). But we need not embrace occasionalism to realize that our very existence is dependent upon God. The doctrines of creation and conservation are sufficient for that.

4.2 Embracing Dependence

Earlier, I indicated that these three kinds of dependence are related. Clearly, if one endorses a theological view according to which all of creation is dependent upon God for its continued existence, then the other two types of dependence are rooted in the kinds of beings that God created and sustains us as. Apart from a theological framework such as those already discussed, one may hold that neither physical nor social dependence entails dependence on God. But they do entail each other. Aspects of our physical dependence entail social dependence. We depend upon others to help us satisfy our needs for food, clothing, and shelter. Similarly, human social dependence on emotional support, education, and political community cannot be separated from the kinds of physical bodies we have. All humans have needs that we cannot provide for ourselves. We are dependent in a number of interconnected ways whether we recognize it or not, whether we admit it or not. Much of Western culture values autonomy in such a way that "depending on others for the gestures of everyday life is often felt as an attack on dignity, as an occasion for shame" (Cooreman-Guittin 2021, 4). But there is benefit to recognizing it.

In her recent book *God's Provision, Humanity's Need: The Gift of Dependence*, theologian Christa McKirkland recognizes that there is a "tendency in

Western thinking . . . to strive for self-sufficiency and absolute autonomy. . . . Such striving undermines true flourishing. We were intended to need to relate to God and others" (McKirkland, 4f). Recognizing the limitations that result from our embodiment helps us realize that much in our lives is beyond our control. Theologian Kelly Kapic agrees: "We often hang on to the delusion that if we just work harder, if we simply squeeze tighter, if we become more efficient, we can eventually regain control. We imagine we can keep our children safe, our incomes secure, our bodies whole" (Kapic 2022, 5). While I don't think that many of us actually believe we have the kind of control that Kapic suggests, we do sometimes live as if we did. In contrast, Kapic asserts that "even dependence, contrary to the individualistic philosophy of our culture, is part of the blessing of human existence" (Kapic 2022, 53). Not only can we not avoid human dependence, but it's possible to see it as a good to be embraced. Theologian Talitha Cooreman-Guittin, for instance, refers to the vulnerability that comes from human dependence as "a source of love because it allows us to open ourselves to others" (Cooreman-Guittin 2021, 11). Christian ethicist Sandra Sullivan-Dunbar has traced how our cultural understanding of dependence has shifted from an acknowledged part of the human conditions to having a negative connotation, in part because of the change in thinking about human value and worth that happened in the industrial revolution (see Sullivan-Dunbar 2017, especially chapter 3). Rather than seeking to avoid dependence, then, we should figure out how best to respond to human dependence, both in ourselves and in others. Eva Kittay, drawing on Margret Baltes' work (Baltes 1995), refers to this as the project of "managing dependency" (Kittay 2019).

None of this discussion, however, means that all forms of human dependence are good. Psychology has shown that certain forms of codependence can be extremely damaging for human well-being and relationships. But the possibility of problematic dependence relationships doesn't alter the fundamental fact that to be human is to be dependent in a number of ways. Given our dependence, we have needs that must be met by others. What follows from this fact? Many feminist philosophers think that human dependence has significant importance for how we think about ethics. (Sandra Sullivan-Dunbar argues that Christian ethics can learn from feminist work in philosophical ethics; see Sullivan-Dunbar 2017.) Sarah Clark Miller, for instance, writes that "some needs [such as fundamental needs] have undeniable normative force" (Miller 2012, 15). The same is also true of embodiment: There is normative force to having bodies of the sort we do. Bodies that differ in important ways also may have different normative pull on others. Those who are immunocompromised or suffer from chronic fatigue or pain, for instance, might need different treatment than those who are healthy. But fundamentally humans have the same needs, even if there is a range of ways those needs can be met. In the last section of this Element, we'll briefly examine some of the moral issues that arise from human embodiment and dependence.

5 Embodiment, Need, and Care

Given our embodiment, finitude and dependence are unavoidable aspects of human nature. The previous sections have sought to undermine a number of misconceptions about various kinds of human embodiment that tend to be stigmatized and devalued. Feminists have long argued that what we think about bodies, and what we expect them to be like, is not normatively neutral. Expectations shape treatment. Eva Kittay reminds us that "we need to come to grips with the ease with which dependency comes to be despised and stigmatized, particularly within an ideology shaped by the image of the independent citizen and amplified when other forms of dependency take on a [negative] characterological aspect" (Kittay 2019, 151). Given these larger value judgments that shape how we think about various kinds of bodies and dependence, certain especially stigmatized forms have been taken to exclude people from the moral community (see McMahan and Singer 2017 for one such example). But rather than just arguing that various kinds of deviant embodiments need to be more valued, this Element also seeks to argue that consideration of the range of human embodiment can help us better understand some of the ethical demands that we confront.

Becoming aware of the various kinds of dependence that come from human embodiment, either our own or that of others, can change the kind of people we are and what we value. It can also change what we think about how we should structure our social lives. Barbara Schmitz thinks that by paying attention to the demands resulting from embodiment, "we might become aware that dependency and vulnerability can be valuable for us," (Schmitz 2014, 71) especially as part of the overall human experience. (Mackenzie et al. 2014a contains a good discussion of the concept of vulnerability.) I begin this final section with an examination of how our dependence results in various needs, which in turn require care if they are to be met.

5.1 Dependence and Fundamental Needs

Issues related to the moral significance of human need and dependence have been pushed to the margins of much ethical reflection. As Sarah Clark Miller argues in her book *The Ethics of Need*, as a result of this comparative neglect, "certain vital aspects of our shared humanity have remained inadequately theorized and, as a result, have been misconstrued" (Miller 2012, 2). In the abstract, it is not contentious that others' needs exact an ethical pull on us. We should seek to meet others' needs, especially if we take seriously the demands of love for our neighbors. Miller argues that when seeking to meet needs, we need to do so accurately not abstractly, giving consideration to the particularities that arise from actual lived experience. Such consideration shows us that needs can conflict, and further reflection is required in order to figure out how to adjudicate between competing needs. Not all needs are equal, so we must at the least prioritize more important over less important needs. The most important needs are what Miller calls "fundamental needs." A fundamental need is a need that

> must be met for a person (1) to avoid significant harm; (2) to be able to choose and carry out action in the world; and (3) to be self-determining. Fundamental needs arise in situations or conditions in which the agency (or the potential for agency) of an individual is acutely endangered. They are fundamental in that such needs must be met in for an individual to develop, maintain, or reestablish agency. (Miller 2012, 4).

Theologian Christa McKirland gives a slightly different account of the nature of fundamental needs. For her, "fundamental need is that which is necessary for the flourishing of a certain entity and cannot be separated from the constitution of that entity" (McKirland 2022, 136). Despite this difference in definition, both approaches stress that fundamental needs are the most important needs that must be met given the kinds of beings we are, both biologically and socially. Miller continues that "fundamental needs highlight two related aspects of finitude present in all human lives: *vulnerability* and *dependency*. . . . Our vulnerability and dependency, however, are not simply matters of biological fact [though they are that]: both are exacerbated and ameliorated by social processes" (Miller 2012, 37).

Fundamental needs result from aspects of human dependence that are unavoidable given our embodiment. Some fundamental needs are closely related to our physical dependence. Among our fundamental needs are the physical needs for oxygen, basic nutrition, rest, shelter, and bodily integrity. Given the social dimensions of human nature already mentioned, Miller thinks social needs too can be fundamental, even if less often realized to be so. These include the needs for belonging, social recognition, education, or emotional attachment. Unlike desires, fundamental needs are objective and universally applicable to all humans, even if the way those needs are expressed and met vary. None of us can complete long-term projects if we are starving, for instance. However, the best way for a fundamental need to be met might vary from person to person. Some might need to get their nutrition via a g-tube, while others are able to eat via mastication and swallowing.

Miller's account of fundamental needs includes the claim that if our fundamental needs are not met, we won't be able to fully develop or maintain human agency. By "agency" in this context she means "the ability to achieve some manner of results in the world, to affect change in accordance with one's volition, and to maintain the ability to carry out projects" (Miller 2012, 24). The degree of our agency fluctuates over time given factors like age, illness, and various disabilities. This fluctuation is "rooted in human vulnerability and finitude [and] reminds us that we are embodied creatures, necessarily beholden to the limits of lifespan, location, and limb" (Miller 2012, 26). (This fluctuation is one reason that the narrow sense of vulnerability, explained in Section 5.2, is important.)

Miller further argues that due to human finitude, it is inevitable that individuals' fundamental needs will at times be in jeopardy. All humans are both vulnerable and dependent, both biologically and socially. We can't always be sure that our fundamental needs will be met because we are not able to meet all of our needs on our own. On such occasions, others must help meet these needs if we are to continue to function as the kinds of agents we are. Since all of us will face moments when there is risk that our fundamental needs will not be met, we find ourselves in a condition of mutual dependence on others in the moral community. Here, she argues, we encounter the "requirement for moral agents to tend to others' fundamental needs by cultivating, maintaining, or restoring the agency of those in need" (Miller 2012, 7). This tending to the fundamental needs of others she calls "care."

5.2 Vulnerability

The concept of vulnerability is closely related to that of need. Etymologically, vulnerability comes from the Latin word *vulnus*, for "wound." On this understanding, vulnerability is rooted in the capacity to be wounded or suffer inherent to human embodiment. Sometimes vulnerability brings with it negative connotations of helplessness, victimhood, or pathology (Mackenzie 2014, 33). However, I think it's better to understand vulnerability as part of the ontological condition of our embodiment. Drawing on the work of Susan Dodds, we can understand vulnerability as "arising from our embodiment and the risk of harm or failure to flourish that follow from that embodiment" (Dodds 2014, 188). Dependence, on her view, is a subcategory of vulnerability that requires the support of other persons – that is, it requires care. Philosophers such as Alysdair MacIntyre and Martha Nussbaum connect vulnerability not only to our bodies' capacity for injury or the failure to flourish but also to the inherent social nature of human life: "As embodied, social beings, we are both vulnerable to the actions of others and dependent on the care and support of other people – to varying degrees at various points in our lives. . . . Vulnerability and dependency are thus intertwined" (Mackenzie et al. 2014b, 4).

Some forms of vulnerability are inherent to the human condition, such as the possibility of becoming ill or dying. Curt Thompson says that vulnerability, in this sense, is not something that happens to us at moments, "[r]ather, it is something we *are*. . . . To be human *is* to be vulnerable" (Thompson 2015, 120). Other forms of vulnerability, such as homelessness, the increased chance of ill health due to poverty, or those associated with the Ugly Laws already discussed, are situational (see Mackenzie et al. 2014b, 7 and Mackenzie 2014, 38f). Paul Formosa calls the former sense in which to be human entails being vulnerable the "broad sense" of vulnerability, and the way that some people or populations are more susceptible to harms at certain times than others given facts about them that are not shared by all humans the "narrow sense" of vulnerability (Formosa 2014, 91). The broad sense involves any degree of vulnerability that arises from our embodied nature, while the narrow sense of vulnerability varies to a great degree among individuals and subpopulations. We are not equally vulnerable in the narrow sense. Aspects of our vulnerability change over time given facts about our physical bodies and social connections. Inequality of resources, power, or need make some agents more vulnerable than others. While we can't eliminate vulnerability in the broad sense, we can and should take steps to reduce many instances of inequalities with respect to the latter.

Some scholars (e.g., Eva Kittay and Martha Nussbaum) think that moral obligations arise directly from vulnerability. Others (e.g., Catriona Mackenzie, Wendy Rogers, and Susan Dodds) don't think that moral obligations are directly rooted in vulnerability. They instead think that vulnerability helps us recognize obligations that come from other moral claims. On this second and weaker view, the normative significance of vulnerability is alerting us to the moral requirement to care for others, even if the obligation is not grounded in the vulnerability itself. Even on this weaker view, vulnerability is something that we should consider for the sake of understanding our ethical lives.

Alysdair MacIntyre's *Dependent Rational Animals*, for instance, is an influential examination of the "virtues that we need, if we are to confront and respond to vulnerability and disability both in ourselves and in others" (MacIntyre 1999, 5). Vulnerability and dependence, for MacIntyre, are central to the human condition as embodied. He insists not only are there virtues that should perfect our giving of care to those who are dependent upon us but that there are also virtues that perfect our receiving the same from others, such as the virtue of exhibiting gratitude toward others. MacIntyre refers to these virtues as "the virtues of acknowledged dependence." A central trust of *Dependent Rational Animals* is that given human vulnerability, the right sort of environment is needed for humans to flourish. The goods for individuals in a particular community are closely connected with, rather than in competition with, the goods of their fellow community members. "The goods to be achieved are neither mine-rather-than-others' nor others'-rather-than-mine, but are instead goods that can only be insofar as they are also those of others, that are genuinely common goods, as the goods of networks of givens and receiving are" (MacIntyre 1999, 119). The wrongs that come from the failure to provide the opportunities needed for flourishing arise from two sources: "One is individual moral failing, arising from the vices of someone's character. The others is found in the systemic flaws of some particular set of social relationships in which the relationships or giving and receiving are embedded" (MacIntyre 1999, 101f). The second source arises when an agent's social environment isn't responsive to their particular narrow vulnerability. While the two sources of failure to provide for flourishing are not unrelated, it is possible for one to arise without the other. Merely having good individual intentions and virtues, apart from the kinds of social structures that can properly provide what people need given their vulnerability and dependence, cannot guarantee human flourishing. We must, MacIntyre argues, think about structure. Both vulnerability and the flourishing it can make precarious are social in nature.

5.3 Caring in Light of Fundamental Dependence

We can think of care as those activities undertaken to meet the needs, especially the fundamental needs, of others. Care, so understood, is a moral response to ineliminable human vulnerability. For those who are religiously motivated, the importance of care for those who are dependent can be understood as an outworking of the love to which we care called (see Sullivan-Dunbar 2017). While care work can perhaps at time increase autonomy and independence, the goal shouldn't be seen as eliminating dependence (see Fineman 2004). That can't be done. The goal should be helping the recipients to flourish or have increased well-being.

In her work on the ethics of care, feminist philosopher Eva Feder Kittay notes that there is a sense in which we think of care as a success term. That is, there's a normative sense of the word care that picks out "care as it ought to be practiced if it is to do what care is supposed to do" (Kittay 2019, 137). Care work, even if sincerely aimed at providing for the best interests of those needing care, often fails to benefit. And in far too many cases, it actually harms others. Kittay uses small caps CARE to point out this normative sense of the term.

We can then also think of misguided care, attempts to provide CARE that don't actually succeed in helping meet the needs of the cared-for, as "mere" or "misguided" care. In this way, CARE can be understood as the called for moral response to others' needs.

Kittay develops an "ethic of care," where the practices of CARE are "themselves a source of normativity" (Kittay 2019, 169). She summarizes the definitions and principles that form the regulative ideals of such as ethic as follows:

> Definition 1: The *telos* of caring practices is the flourishing of those who are in need of care.
> Definition 2: Those who are in need of care are those who will be harmed if care is not provided.
> Principle 1. The *regulative ideals* of care are to provide care by assisting those who require care
>
> (a) in meeting the genuine needs (that is, needs that have both an objective and a subjective basis).
> (b) in meeting the legitimate wants (that is, wants that can be satisfied without thwarting another's possibility to receive the care another – including the carer – may require).
>
> Principle 2. The flourishing of those in need of care has to be a flourishing as endorsed (implicitly or explicitly) by the one cared for. (Kittay 2019, 139)

Kittay's regulative ideals of care don't perfectly align with Miller's work. While Miller focuses on fundamental needs, defined in Section 5.1, Kittay focuses on genuine needs. For Kittay, genuine needs are those needs that will impede the flourishing of the individual in question if not met, and thus are a broader set of needs than Miller's category of fundamental needs. In addition to genuine needs, Kittay thinks that flourishing also depends on the satisfaction of legitimate wants, which are desires that can be met without sacrificing the genuine needs or legitimate wants of others.

Also note that Kittay's Principle 2 is included specifically to avoid cases of paternalism. CARE, for Kittay, is "fundamentally opposed to a paternalistic imposition of a putative objective conception of a person's good" over that person's legitimate wants (Kittay 2019, 201). Questions of paternalism, especially in the context of caring for those with disabilities as Kittay's work does, are complex. History is full of cases where paternalistic action in the attempt to care for others' embodiment has gone very wrong. This history includes the institutionalization of individuals with disabilities, many of whom would be abused in such institutions, myopic focus on BMI as a marker of a person's health, or even medical providers engaged in acts of "mercy killing." If we are to successfully love others, especially those who are particularly vulnerable, we should seek to ensure that we are providing CARE rather than perpetuating unintended harms.

Receiving care can thus be risky, especially if the relevant actions don't succeed in providing CARE. But the same is also true of providing care, especially in a society where the expectations and resources for providing care work track other dimensions of social position. Giving care can increase the situational vulnerability of the carer (see Kittay 1998 and Nishida 2022 for discussions of such risks).

Recognizing our need to both receive and give care is important but not sufficient. Such recognition doesn't solve some of the hard moral questions about CARE, including the following:

- Who should provide CARE, and to whom? (see Mackenzie et al. 2014a)
- What exact form(s) should caregiving take?
- What principles should govern specifics of how we give and receive CARE?
- How do we balance competing fundamental needs in light of limited resources, including time?
- How can we balance the needs of those giving CARE with the needs of those receiving it?
- How can we prevent the providing of CARE from falling disproportionately on marginalized and disenfranchised groups?

These issues, and others, warrant further exploration. But regardless of how these questions are best answered, we need to keep in mind that we are not all vulnerable in the same ways and to the same degrees. This, again, is the narrow sense of vulnerability introduced in Section 5.1. Often, those who will benefit the most from having good structures of care will be those with the highest degree of the narrow sense of vulnerability. In this way, to draw on MacIntyre again, these individuals reveal something about the goodness of the community as a whole given their increased vulnerability: "The very young and the very old, the sick, the injured, and the otherwise disabled, and their individual flourishing will be an important index of the flourishing of the whole community. For it is insofar as it is *need* that provides reasons for action for the members of some particular community that the community flourishes" (MacIntyre 1999, 108f).

Along a similar line, Martha Fineman argues that the obligation to engage in caregiving is not just borne individually, but socially: "a sense of social justice demands a broader sense of obligation [than merely from the cared-for to their care-givers]. Without aggregate caretaking, there could be no society, so we might say that it is caretaking labour that produces and reproduces society" (Fineman 2000, 19f). But given, as already argued, we're all socially dependent on others for our own well-being, we all thus benefit from the labor that sustains our societies. Structuring our communities to better be able to meet these needs will require us to rethink not only the distribution of care responsibilities but also our labor and economic structures. Marta Russell's work, for instance, argues that much disability oppression is rooted in capitalism such that exploitation of disabled people is an inextricable constituent of contemporary capitalism (Russell 2019).

5.4 Conclusion

There is tremendous pressure to think of ourselves as more independent than we are. Susan Dodds notes that overly individualistic or atomistic views of autonomy not only fail to recognize the various dimensions of human dependence but can also increase the risk of exploitation, disadvantage, and devaluing members of the human moral community. She argues that

> attention to *vulnerability* . . . changes citizens' ethical relations from those of independent actors carving out realms of right against each other and the state, to those of mutually-dependent and vulnerability-exposed beings whose capacities to develop as subjects are directly and indirectly mediated by the conditions around them. (Dodds 2007, 501; see also Anderson 2014 and Sullivan-Dunbar 2017, chapter 3)

Much of contemporary society acts as if a level of independence that isn't actually achievable is the norm. Think, for instance, of the myth of the self-made millionaire who is dependent on no other individual for their wealth. But none of us is independent. Recognizing this will lead to a "change in the way we look at dependent persons goes far beyond the framework of medicine or organized care and should involve society as a whole, because politics, media, economy and even churches are profoundly influenced by the conception of autonomy and independence as the ultimate guarantors of people's dignity" (Cooreman-Guittin 2021, 5). Eva Kittay notes that "in our modern industrial and postindustrial world, where independence is construed as the mark of adulthood, it is difficult for many to acknowledge that dependency may be a permanent feature of life, and that dependency can recur (to various degrees and in different ways) throughout our lives, so that we are always vulnerable to once again becoming fully dependent" (Kittay 2019, 147).

Recognizing the dependence and vulnerability that arise from our embodiment gives us reason to work to bring about and support the kinds of institutions and social structures that will contribute to our flourishing. Here again we encounter the danger of problematic forms of paternalism and other complex questions (see Mackenzie 2014, Section 2). Nevertheless, we should work so that our social structures and relationships equip us to flourish as the kinds of embodied agents that we are.

References

Amy, N. K., Aalborg, A., Lyons, P., & Keranen, L. (2006). Barriers to routine gynecological cancer screening for white and African-American obese women. *International Journal of Obesity*, *30*(1), 147–155.

Anderson, J. (2014). Autonomy and vulnerability entwined. In C. Mackenzie, W. Rogers, & S. Dodds (Eds.), *Vulnerability: New essays in ethics and feminist philosophy* (pp. 134–161). Oxford: Oxford University Press.

Aristotle. (2017). *Politics* (trans. Benjamin Jowett, Ed.). New York: Digireads.

Baltes, M. M. (1995). Dependency in old age: Gains and losses. *Current Directions in Psychological Science*, *4*(1), 14–19.

Balwin, J. (1992). *The fire next time*. New York: Vintage.

Barnes, E. (2016). *The minority body: A theory of disability*. Oxford: Oxford University Press.

Baynton, D. (2001). Disability and the justification of inequality in American history. In P. K. Longmore, & L. Umansky (Eds.), *The new disability history: American perspectives* (pp. 33–57). New York: New York University Press.

Beaudoin, J. (2007). The world's continuance: Divine conservation or existential inertia? *International Journal for Philosophy of Religion*, *61*, 83–98.

Bowen-Evans, K. (2022). How Brian Brock's hermeneutic of disability is relevant to all marginalsed bodies. *Journal of Disability & Religion*, *26*(2), 165–175.

Bowman Jr., D. (2021). *On the spectrum: Autism, faith, & the gifts of neuodiversity*. Grand Rapids, MI: Brazos Press.

Boyer, A. (2019). *The undying*. New York: Farrar, Strause and Giroux.

Bynum, C. W. (1995). *The resurrection of the body in western christianity, 200–1336*. New York: Columbia University Press.

Byrom, B. (2004). *A vision of self support: Disability and the rehabilitation movement of progressive America*. Iowa City: University of Iowa.

Campbell, S. M., & Stramondo, J. A. (2017). The complicated relationship of disability and well-being. *Kennedy Institute of Ethics Journal*, *27*(2), 151–184.

Carel, H. (2019). *Illness: The cry of the flesh* (3rd ed.). New York: Routledge.

Chambers, C. (2022). *Intact: A defence of the unmodified body*. Milton Keynes: Allen Lane.

Chatzidakis, A., Hakim, J., Littler, J., Rottenberg, C., & Segal, L. (2020). *The care manifesto: The politics of interdependence*. London: Verso.

Chouinard, V. (1997). Making space for disabling differenced: Challenging ableist geographies. *Environment and Planning D: Society and Space*, *15*(4), 379–387.

Clare, E. (2017). *Brilliant imperfection: Grappling with cure*. Durham, NC: Duke University Press.

Clark-Soles, J. (2017). John, first – third john, and revelation. In S. J. Melcher, M. C. Parsons, & A. Yong (Eds.), *The bible and disability: A commentary* (pp. 333–378). Waco, TX: Baylor University Press.

Connolly, M. (2001). Female embodiment and clinical practice. In S. K. Toombs (Ed.), *Handbook of phenomenology and medicine* (pp. 177–196). Dordrecht: Kluwer Academic.

The cooperative human. (2018). *Nature Human Behavior*, *2*, 427–428. www.nature.com/articles/s41562-018-0389-1.

Cooreman-Guittin, T. (2021). Looking at dependence: Vulnerability and power in the gospel of the foot washing. *Journal of Disability & Religion*, *25*(1), 4–14.

Crisp, O. D., & Strobel, K. C. (2018). *Jonathan Edwards: An introduction to his thought*. Grand Rapids, MI: Wm. B. Eerdmans.

Dea, S. (2016). *Beyond the binary: Thinking about sex and gender*. Peterborough, CA: Broadview Press.

Descartes, R. (1993). *Meditations on first philosophy* (trans. Donald A. Cross, Ed.). Indianapolis, IN: Hackett.

Dodds, S. (2007). Depending on care: Recognition of vulnerability and the social contribution of care provision. *Bioethics*, *21*(9), 500–510.

Dodds, S. (2014). Dependence, care, and vulnerability. In C. Mackenzie, W. Rogers, & S. Dodds (Eds.), *Vulnerability: New essays in ethics and feminist philosophy* (pp. 181–203). Oxford: Oxford University Press.

Dyke, C. V. (2020). Taking the "dis" out of disability: Martyrs, mothers, and mystics in the middle ages. In S. M. Williams (Ed.), *Disability in medieval christian philosophy and theology* (pp. 203–232). New York: Routledge.

Eyler, J. R. (2010). Introduction: Breaking boundaries, building bridges. In J. R. Eyler (Ed.), *Disability in the middle ages: Reconsiderations and reverberations* (pp. 1–8). New York: Routledge.

Fessenden, T. (1999). The soul of America: Whiteness and the disappearing of bodies in the progressive era. In G. Weiss, & H. F. Haber (Eds.), *Perspectives on embodiment: The intersections of nature and culture* (pp. 23–40). New York: Routledge.

Fineman, M. (2000). Cracking the foundational myths: Independence, autonomy and self-sufficiency. *American University Journal of Gender, Social Policy, & the Law*, *8*(13), 12–29.

Fineman, M. (2004). *The autonomy myth: A theory of dependency*. New York: New Press.

Fisher, S. (1973). *Body consciousness: You are what you feel*. Englewood Cliffs, NJ: Prentice Hall.

Flint, S. W. (2015). Obesity stigma: Prevalence and impact in healthcare. *British Journal of Obesity*, *1*, 14–18.

Formosa, P. (2014). The role of vulnerabiliby in Kantian ethics. In C. Mackenzie, W. Rogers, & S. Dodds (Eds.), *Vulnerability: New essays in ethics and feminist philosophy* (pp. 88–109). Oxford: Oxford University Press.

Frye, M. (1983). Oppression. In *Politics of reality: Essays in feminist theory* (pp. 1–16). New York: Crossing Press.

Gaudet, M. (2017). On "and vulnerable": Catholic social thought and the social challenges of cognitive disability. *Journal of Moral Theology*, *6*(2), 52–53.

Glenn, E. N. (2010). *Forced to care: Coercion and caregiving in America*. Cambridge, MA: Harvard University Press.

Gordon, A. (2020). *What we don't talk about when we talk about fat*. Boston, MA: Beacon Press.

Grimes, K. W. (2016). *Christ divided: Antiblackness as corporate vice*. Minneapolis, MN: Fortress Press.

Grue, J. (2023, March 14). *The disabled villain: Why sensitivity reading can't kill off this ugly trope*. Retrieved March 14, 2023, from www.theguardian.com/news/2023/mar/14/the-disabled-villain-why-sensitivity-reading-cant-kill-off-this-ugly-trope

Hahn, H. (1995). The appearance of physical difference: A new agenda for research on politics and disability. *Journal of Health and Human Services Administration*, *17*(4), 391–415.

Hall, S. S., MacMichael, J., & Turner, A. (2017). A survey of the impact of owning a service dog on quality of life for individuals with physical and hearing disability: A pilot study. *Health and Quality of Life Outcomes*, *15*(1), 59.

Hamermesh, D. S., & Biddle, J. E. (1993). Beauty and the labour market. *National Bureau of Economic Research Paper Series, working paper 4518*, 1–46.

Hardy, K. A. (2023). Five ways health care can be better for fat people. *AMA Journal of Ethics*, *25*(7), 528–534.

Harris, J. E. (2019). The aesthetics of disability. *Columbia Law Review*, *119*(4), 895–971.

Hehir, T. (2002). Eliminating ableism in education. *Harvard Educational Review*, *72*(1), 1–33.

Heyes, C. J. (2021). The body. In K. Q. Hall, & Ásta (Eds.), *The oxford handbook of feminist philosophy* (pp. 350–362). Oxford: Oxford University Press.

Holcomb, J., & Latham-Mintus, K. (2022). Disney and disability: Media representations of disability in Disney and Pixar animated films. *Disability Studies Quarterly*, *42*(1).

Holmes, K. (2020). *Mismatch: How inclusion shapes design*. Cambridge, MA: MIT Press.

House, S. (1981). A radical feminist model of psychological disability. *Off Our Backs*, *11*(5), 34–35.

Huebner, B. (2016). Review of *Cognitive Pluralism*, by Steven Horst. *Notre Dame Philosophical Reviews*. Retrieved Feburary 1, 2023, from https://ndpr.nd.edu/reviews/cognitive-pluralism/

Jacobs, A. E. (2023). How body mass index comprises care of patients with disabilities. *AMA Journal of Ethics*, *25*(7), 545–549.

Kapic, K. M. (2022). *You're only human*. Grand Rapids, MI: Brazos Press.

Kaposy, C. (2018). *Choosing down syndrome: Ethics and new prenatal testing technologies*. Cambridge, MA: MIT Press.

Kaposy, C. (2019). The ethical line for down syndrome testing. *Policy Options*. Retrieved April 25, 2023, from https://policyoptions.irpp.org/magazines/april-2019/the-ethical-line-for-down-syndrome-testing/

Kenney, E. L., Gortmaker, S. L., Davison, K. K., & Bryn Austin, S. (2015). The academic penalty for gaining weight: A longitudinal, change-in-change analysis of BMI and perceived academic ability in middle school students. *International Journal of Obesity*, *39*, 1408–1409.

Kenny, A. (2022). *My body is not a prayer request: Disability justice in the church*. Grand Rapids, MI: Brazos Press.

Kittay, E. F. (1998). *Love's labor: Essays on women, equality, and dependence*. New York: Routledge.

Kittay, E. F. (2019). *Learning from my daughter: The value and care of disabled minds*. New York: Oxford University Press.

Kristiva, J. (1982). *Powers of horror: An essay on abjection* (trans. Leon S. Roudiez, Ed.). New York: Columbia University Press.

Kukla, Q. R. (2009). The phrenological impulse and the morphology of character. In S. Campbell, L. Meynell, & S. Sherwin (Eds.), *Embodiment and agency* (pp. 76–99). University Park: The Pennsylvania State University Press.

Kukla, Q. R. (2022). What counts as a disease, and why does it matter? *The Journal of Philosophy of Disability*, 2, 1–27.

Kumari Campbell, F. (2009). *Countours of ableism: The production of disability and abledness*. New York: Palgrave MacMillan.

Kvanvig, J. L., & McCann, H. J. (1988). Divine conservation and the persistence of the world. In T. V. Morris (Ed.), *Divine and human actions: Essays in the metaphysics of theism* (pp. 13–49). Ithaca, NY: Cornell University Press.

Leder, D. (1990). *The absent body*. Chicago, IL: University of Chicago Press.

Leduc, A. (2020). *Disfigured: On fairy tales, disability, and making space.* Toronto: Coach House Books.

Lehrer, R. (2020). *Golem girl: A memoir*. New York: One World.

Leporrier, N., Herrou, M., Morello, R., & Leymarie, P. (2003). Fetuses with down's syndrome detected by prenatal screening are more likely to abort spontaneously than fetuses with down's syndrome not detected by prenatal screening. *BJOG*, *110*(1), 18–21.

Lewis, T. A. (2020). Ableism: An updated definition. www.talilalewis.com/blog/ableism-2020-an-updated-definition.

Linton, D. (2013). The menstrual masquerade. In J. A. Brune, & D. J. Wilson (Eds.), *Disability and passing: Blurring the lines of identity* (pp. 58–70). Philadelphia, PA: Temple University Press.

Lorde, A. (1980). *The cancer journals*. New York: Penguin Books.

MacIntyre, A. (1999). *Dependent rational animals: Why human beings need the virtues*. Peru, IL: Carus.

Mackenzie, C. (2014). The importance of relational autonomy and capabilities for an ethics of vulnerability. In C. Mackenzie, W. Rogers, & S. Dodds (Eds.), *Vulnerability: New essays in ethics and feminist philosophy* (pp. 33–59). Oxford: Oxford University Press.

Mackenzie, C., Rogers, W., & Dodds, S. (Eds.). (2014a). *Vulnerability: New essays in ethics and feminist philosophy*. Oxford: Oxford University Press.

Mackenzie, C., Rogers, W., & Dodds, S. (2014b). What is vulnerability, and why does it matter for moral theory? In C. Mackenzie, W. Rogers, & S. Dodds (Eds.), *Vulnerability: New essays in ethics and feminist philosophy* (pp. 1–29). Oxford: Oxford University Press.

Manne, K. (2024). *Unshrinking: How to face fatphobia*. New York: Crown.

Martin, A. (2017). 49 states legally allow employers to discriminate based on weight. *Time*.

McGee, S. (2014). *For women, being 13 pounds overweight means losing $9,000 a year in salary.* Retrieved July 14, 2023, from www.theguardian.com/money/us-money-blog/2014/oct/30/women-pay-get-thin-study

McGuire, A. (2016). *War on autism: On the cultural logic of normative violence.* Ann Arbor: University of Michigan Press.

McKirland, C. L. (2022). *God's provision, humanity's need: The gift of our dependence*. Grand Rapids, MI: Baker Academic.

McMahan, J., & Singer, P. (2017, April 3). Who is the victim in the anna stubblefield case? *The New York Times*.

McRuer, R. (2006). *Crip theory: Cultural signs of queerness and disability*. New York: New York University Press.

Melcher, S. J. (2017). Introduction. In S. J. Melcher, M. C. Parsons, & A. Yong (Eds.), *The bible and disability: A commentary* (pp. 1–27). Waco, TX: Baylor University Press.

Metzler, I. (2005). *Disability in medieval Europe: Thinking about physical impairment in the high middle ages, c. 1100–c.1400*. New York: Routledge.

Meynell, L. (2009). Introduction: Minding bodies. In S. Campbell, L. Meynell, & S. Sherwin (Eds.), *Embodiment and agency* (pp. 1–21). University Park: The Pennsylvania State University Press.

Miller, S. C. (2012). *The ethics of need: Agency, dignity, and obligation*. New York: Routledge.

Millgram, E. (2022). Bounded agency. In L. Ferrero (Ed.), *The Routledge handbook of philosophy of agency* (pp. 68–76). New York: Routledge.

Mills, J. S., Shannon, A., & Hogue, J. (2017). Beauty, body image, and the media. In M. P. Levine (Ed.), *Perception of beauty* (pp. 145–157). London: Intechopen.

Mitchell, D. T. (1999). Foreword. In H.- J. Stiker (Ed.), *A History of Disability* (pp. vii–xiv). Ann Arbor: University of Michigan Press.

Mizrahi, M. (2019). If analytic philosophy of religion is sick, can it be cured? *Religious Studies*, *56*(4), 558–577.

Mollow, A. (2022). Hunger always wins: Contesting the medicalization of fat bodies. In J. M. Reynolds, & C. Wieseler (Eds.), *The disability bioethics reader* (pp. 254–262). New York: Routledge.

Murray, S. (2008). *The "fat" female body*. New York: Palgrave MacMillan.

Natoli, J. L., Ackerman, D. L., McDermott, S., & Edwards, J. G. (2012). Prenatal diagnosis of down syndrome: A systematic review of termination rates (1995–2011). *Prenatal Diagnosis*, *32*(2), 142–153.

Nishida, A. (2022). *Just care: Messy entanglements of disability, dependency, and desire*. Philadelphia, PA: Temple University Press.

Pfeifer, C. (2012). Physical attractiveness, employment and earnings. *Applied Economics Letters*, *19*(6), 505–510.

Phelan, S. M., Burgess, D. J., Yeazel, M. W., et al. (2015). Impact of weight bias and stigma on quality of care and outcomes for patients with obesity. *Obesity Reviews*, *16*(4), 319–326.

Phelan, S. M., Dovidio, J. F., Puhl, R. M., et al. (2014). Implicit and explicit weight bias in a national sample of 4,732 medical students: The medical student changes study. *Obesity*, *22*(4), 1201–1208.

Plato. (2002). *Five dialogues: Euthryphro, Apoogy, Crito, Meno, Phaedo* (trans. G. M. A. Grube, Ed.). Indianapolis, IN: Hackett.

Ratliffe, M. (2008). Touch and situatedness. *International Journal of Philosophical Studies*, *16*(3), 299–322.

Reiheld, A. (2015). With all due caution: Global anti-obesity campaigns and the individualization of responsibility. *International Journal of Feminist Approaches to Bioethics*, *8*(2), 226–249.

Reynolds, J. M. (2022). *The life worth living: Disability, pain, and morality.* Minneapolis: University of Minnesota Press.

Rubino, F., Puhl, R. M., Cummings, D. E., et al. (2020). Joint international consensus statement for ending stigma of disability. *Nature Medicine*, *26*, 485–497.

Russell, M. (2019). *Capitalism & disability: Selected writings by Martha Russell* (K. Rosenthal, Ed.). Chicago, IL: Haymarket Books.

Saguy, A. C. (2013). *What's wrong with fat.* New York: Oxford University Press.

Salim, E., & Malik, S. A. (2022). *Creatio Continua* and quantum randomness. In K. J. Clark, & J. Koperski (Eds.), *Abrahamic reflections on randomness and providence* (pp. 243–264). New York: Springer.

Schmitz, B. (2014). "something else?"–cognitive disability and the human form of life. In J. E. Bickenbach, F. Felder, & B. Schmitz (Eds.), *Disability and the good human life* (pp. 50–71). New York: Cambridge University Press.

Schweik, S. M. (2009). *The ugly laws: Disability in public.* New York: New York University Press.

Scott, E. (2001). Unpicking a myth: The infanticide of female and disabled infants in antiquity. In G. Davies, A. Gardner, & K. Lockyear (Eds.), *Trac 2000: Proceedings of the tenth annual theoretical roman archaeology conference* (pp. 143–151). Oxford: Oxbow Books.

Scully, J. L. (2014). Disability and vulnerability: On bodies, dependence, and power. In C. Mackenzie, W. Rogers, & S. Dodds (Eds.), *Vulnerability: New essays in ethics and feminist philosophy* (pp. 204–221). Oxford: Oxford University Press.

Shakespeare, T. (2014). Nasty, brutish, and short? On the predicament of disability and embodiment. In J. E. Bickenbach, F. Felder, & B. Schmitz (Eds.), *Disability and the good human life* (pp. 93–112). Cambridge: Cambridge University Press.

Shapiro, J. P. (1994). *No pity*. New York: Three Rivers Press.

Siebers, T. (2003). What can disability studies learn from the culture wars? *Cultural Critique*, *55*, 182–216.

Sierminska, E. (2015). Does it pay to be beautiful? *IZA World of Labor*, 161.

Simmons, J. A. (2019). The strategies of christian philosophy. In J. A. Simmons (Ed.), *Christian philosophy: Conceptions, continuations, and challenges* (pp. 187–207). Oxford: Oxford University Press.

Smith, J. K. A. (2021). *The nicene option: An incarnational phenomenology*. Waco: Baylor University Press.

Snead, O. C. (2020). *What it means to be human: The case for the body in public bioethics*. Cambridge, MA: Harvard University Press.

Sole-Smith, V. (2023). *Fat talk: Parenting in the age of diet culture*. New York: Henry Hold.

Solomon, A. (2012). *Far from the tree: Parents, children, and the search for identity*. New York: Simon & Schuster.

Stiker, H.- J. (2000). *A history of disability* (trans. William Sayers, Ed.). Ann Arbor: University of Michigan Press.

Suchocki, M. H. (1994). *The fall to violence: Original sin in relational theology* (New York ed.). London: Continuum.

Sullivan-Dunbar, S. (2017). *Human dependency and christian ethics*. Cambridge: Cambridge University Press.

Swartz, K., Lutfiyya, Z. M., & Hansen, N. (2013). Dopey's legacy: Stereotypical portrayals of intellectual disability in the classic animated films. In J. Cheu (Ed.), *Diversity in Disney films: Critical essays on race, ethnicity, gender, sexuality and disability* (pp. 179–194). Jefferson: McFarland.

Swinton, J., Mowat, H., & Baines, S. (2011). Whose story am I? Redescribing profound intellectual disability in the kingdom of god. *Journal of Religion, Disability and Health*, *15*, 5–19.

Taylor, S. R. (2018). *The body is not an apology: The power of radical self-love*. Oakland, CA: Berrett-Koehler.

Thompson, C. (2015). *The soul of shame: Retelling the stories we believe about ourselves*. Downers Grove, IL: InterVarsity Press.

Thomson, R. G. (Ed.). (1996). *Freakery: Cultural spectacles of the extraordinary body*. New York: New York University Press.

Thomson, R. G. (1997). *Extraordinary bodies: Figuring physical disability in American culture and literature*. New York: Columbia University Press.

Timpe, K. (2018). *Disability and inclusive communities*. Grand Rapids, MI: Calvin Press.

Timpe, K. (2020). Defiant afterlife–disability and uniting ourselves to god. In M. Panchuk, & M. C. Rea (Eds.), *Voices from the edge: Centering marginalized perspectives in analytic theology* (pp. 206–231). Oxford: Oxford University Press.

Tomiyama, A. J., Carr, D., Granberg, E. M., et al. (2018). How and why weight stigma drives the obesity "epidemic" and harms health. *BMC Medicine, 16*(123), 1–6.

Toombs, S. K. (2001). Reflections on bodily change: The lived experience of disability. In S. K. Toombs (Ed.), *Handbook of phenomenology and medicine* (pp. 247–262). Dordrecht: Kluwer Academic.

Torrance, A. J. (2022). Foreward. In C. L. McKirland (Ed.), *God's provision, humanity's need: The gift of our dependence* (pp. ix–xii). Grand Rapids, MI: Baker Academic.

Tremain, S. L. (2017). *Foucault and feminist philosophy of disability*. Ann Arbor: University of Michigan Press.

Tylka, T. L., Annunziato, R. A., Burgand, D., et al. (2014). The weight-inclusive vs. weight-normative approach to health: Evaluating the evidence for prioritizing well-being over weight loss. *Journal of Obesity, 2014*, 1–18.

Urla, J., & Terry, J. (1995). Introduction: Mapping embodied deviance. In J. Urla, & J. Terry (Eds.), *Deviant bodies: Critical perspectives on difference in science and popular culture* (pp. 1–18). Bloomington: Indiana University Press.

Van Dyke, C. (2020). Taking the 'Dis' Out of Disability: Martyrs, Mothers, and Mystics. In S. Williams (Ed.), *Disability in Medieval Christian Philosophy and Theology* (pp. 203–232). New York: Routledge.

Van Dyke, C. (2022). *A hidden wisdom: Medieval contemplatives on self-knowledge, reason, love, persons, and immortality*. Oxford: Oxford University Press.

Wallace, D. F. (2009). *This is water*. New York: Little, Brown.

Wangelin, H. (2021). What I wish my parents knew about being their autistic daughter. In E. P. Ballou, S. daVanport, & M. G. Onaiwu (Eds.), *Sincerely, your autistic child* (pp. 31–46). Boston, MA: Beacon Press.

Wendell, S. (1996). *The rejected body: Feminist philosophical reflections on disability*. New York: Routledge.

Wendell, S. (2001). Unhealthy disability: Treating chronic illness as disabilities. *Hypatia, 16*(4), 17–33.

Widdows, H. (2018). *Perfect me: Beauty as an ethical ideal*. Princeton, NJ: Princeton University Press.

Wieseler, C. (2019). Challenging conceptions of the "normal" subject in phenomenology. In E. S. Lee (Ed.), *Race as phenomena: Between phenomenology and philosophy of race* (pp. 69–85). London: Rowman & Littlefield.

Wolf, N. (1991). *The beauty myth*. New York: William Morrow.

Wright, N. (2008). *Surprised by hope*. New York: HarperOne.

Wright, N. (2017, June). History, eschatology and new creation: Early christian perspectives on god's action in Jesus. University of St. Andrews. https://www.youtube.com/watch?v=yf2SJb55iJ0

Wright, N. (2019). *History and eschatology: Jesus and the promise of natural theology*. Waco, TX: Baylor University Press.

Yong, A. (2007). *Theology and Down syndrome: Reimaging disability in late modernity*. Waco, TX: Baylor University Press.

Young, I. M. (1990). *On female body experience: "throwing like a girl."* Oxford: Oxford University Press.

Young, L. M., & Powell, B. (1985). The effects of obesity on the clinical judgments of mental health professionals. *Journal of Health and Social Behaviour*, *26*(3), 234–246.

Young, S. N. (2008). The neurobiology of human social behavior: An important but neglected topic. *Journal of Psychiatric Neuroscience*, *33*(5), 391–392.

Acknowledgments

Much of the work on this Element was completed while I was on a sabbatical from Calvin University during the spring semester of 2023. My colleagues, both within the philosophy department and across campus at Calvin, are a real gift and I am very grateful for their generous and continuing support. Work on this Element also took place while I was in the Chicago Semester Scholar-in-Residence program during the summer of 2022. Both Bronzeville and the Gold Coast are lovely places to write and rejuvenate. While on sabbatical, Burn Boot Camp (Grand Rapids) was an excellent community in which to both enjoy and nurture embodiment. While writing this Element, I was part of a writing co-op and benefitted from support and accountability from Aaron Cobb, Audra Goodnight, and Michelle Panchuk. Thanks to Holly Lillis for encouragement and reminding me that the material in this Element could be valuable to those who have experienced the issues I discuss. (*Fais rage, loutre.*) I am also thankful for all the feminist philosophers I've learned from, both in terms of content and methodology, in recent years and who have shaped how I've approached these topics. Finally, thanks to series editor Michael Peterson for shepherding this Element from initial concept to reality.

Cambridge Elements

The Problems of God

Series Editor

Michael L. Peterson
Asbury Theological Seminary

Michael L. Peterson is Professor of Philosophy at Asbury Theological Seminary. He is the author of *God and Evil* (Routledge); *Monotheism, Suffering, and Evil* (Cambridge University Press); *With All Your Mind* (University of Notre Dame Press); *C. S. Lewis and the Christian Worldview* (Oxford University Press); *Evil and the Christian God* (Baker Book House); and *Philosophy of Education: Issues and Options* (Intervarsity Press). He is co-author of *Reason and Religious Belief* (Oxford University Press); *Science, Evolution, and Religion: A Debate about Atheism and Theism* (Oxford University Press); and *Biology, Religion, and Philosophy* (Cambridge University Press). He is editor of *The Problem of Evil: Selected Readings* (University of Notre Dame Press). He is co-editor of *Philosophy of Religion: Selected Readings* (Oxford University Press) and *Contemporary Debates in Philosophy of Religion* (Wiley-Blackwell). He served as General Editor of the Blackwell monograph series Exploring Philosophy of Religion and is founding Managing Editor of the journal *Faith and Philosophy*.

About the Series

This series explores problems related to God, such as the human quest for God or gods, contemplation of God, and critique and rejection of God. Concise, authoritative volumes in this series will reflect the methods of a variety of disciplines, including philosophy of religion, theology, religious studies, and sociology.

Cambridge Elements

The Problems of God

Elements in the Series

A full series listing is available at: www.cambridge.org/EPOG